Physical Characteristics of the Dogo Argentino
(from the official breed standard)

Body: Topline is highest on withers, smoothly sloping to the croup. Croup is muscular, round, broad and gently sloping. Underline well muscled, with only a slight to moderate tuck-up of the abdomen.

Hindquarters: Broad, with very muscular thighs and short rear pasterns. Normally angulated. Hind legs well apart and parallel.

Tail: Long and thick, tapers down to the hock joint and is set moderately high and smoothly into the croup. Carried curving smoothly upwards, naturally down at rest and always raised while struggling with prey, in continuous lateral movement, as when greeting master.

Color: Completely white.

Size: Height: From 23.6 to 25.6 in (60 to 65 cms), measured at the withers. Weight: From 88.2 to 99.2 lb (40 to 45 kgs).

Coat: Short and thick with a glossy sheen. Hair is stiff, coarse and of uniform length. A field-conditioned coat or working scars should never be faulted.

Feet: Round and compact with short, tight, close-together toes, proportioned to paw size.

Dogo Argentino

by Joseph Janish

Contents

Photographs by:
Norvia Behling, T. J. Calhoun, Carolina Biological Supply, David Dalton, Wil de Veer, Doskocil, Isabelle Français, James Hayden-Yoav, James R. Hayden, RBP, Joseph Janish, Bill Jonas, Linda Kardonis, Dwight R. Kuhn, Dr. Dennis Kunkel, Mikki Pet Products, Phil Owen, Nathalie Pawlak, Phototake, Jean Claude Revy, Alice Roche, Dr. Andrew Spielman, Alice van Kempen and C. James Webb.

The publisher wishes to thank the owners of the dogs featured in this book, including Cheri Carbone, Sandrine Cominotti, Frederique Francois, Laura and Carl Hewitt, Jajome Kennels (D. & J. Carty), Joseph Janish, Linda & John Kardonis, Irene & Clint Knapp, Christian Loviconi, Brent & Misty Moore, Phil Owen, J. van Rijthoven, Tracy Sklenar and Danielle & Brian Szczypinski.

Illustrations by Renée Low.

Kennel Club Books: Dogo Argentino
ISBN: 1-59378-226-8

Copyright © 1999 • Revised American Edition: Copyright © 2003
Kennel Club Books, Inc., 308 Main Street, Allenhurst, NJ 07711 USA
Cover Design Patented: US 6,435,559 B2 • Printed in South Korea

DOGO ARGENTINO

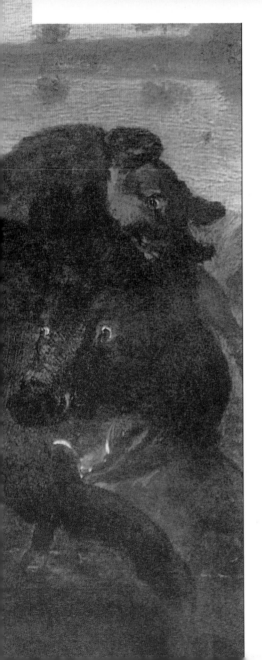

IMAGE OF THE DOGO

Viewed from a distance, the Dogo Argentino strides with great pride, a pure white image of regal power. As the Dogo approaches, the rigid posture and snarling face give an air of determination and courage mixed with "barely contained explosive power." From just a few feet away, distinct musculature ripples through the Dogo's short white hairs. This wonderfully muscular physique and slow, loping gait exudes a confidence that is rarely found in the world of dogs. Leaping gracefully up to you, and standing eye to eye, the Dogo hisses with apparent contempt, smirks at your human visage, then proceeds to gleefully clean your face with his tongue. This is the paradox of the Dogo Argentino: a dog of both unyielding power and the most gentle and loving friendliness.

The ethics of creating a "supermensch" may forever be debated as mankind settles for the stories of Greek gods and comic-book heroes. In the dog world, however, man is allowed to play God, and thus we have the written breed standards by which all dogs are judged. Sometimes the genetic manipulation of man's best friend has been limited to goals of vanity

Reputedly painted in 1635 by Hondius, this painting depicts an ancient mastiff-type dog that bears a similar appearance to the Dogo Argentino. This mastiff was being used to hunt large game such as the wild boar.

and appearance. More often, however, a standard calls for practicality and usefulness to man. Before we can understand the Dogo Argentino, we need to know the background of why the breed was created.

MAN'S SURVIVAL

The natural reality of our world is the survival of the fittest. Man has been fairly successful (so far) in persisting because he is resourceful in fighting the elements and enemies that surround him. Often this resourcefulness extends to the use of others to help his cause. This is where the Dogo Argentino (among others) has come into play. Before we can understand the Dogo, we must understand the Dogo's purpose to man.

In many areas of the world, man's desire to live has been hampered by wild beasts of great strength, speed and size. Throughout Europe, for example, farmland is prone to attacks by wild boar. It seems that no amount of fencing, barbed wire or other barricade can prevent the forceful boars from feasting on the vegetation man has tilled for himself and his domesticated animals. (If you feel that man cannot live on bread alone, consider that the great German winemaker Egon Müller lost almost his entire 1996 harvest to wild boars that devoured his precious Riesling grapes—in spite

of large electrical fences installed to stop them!) These massive demons are responsible not only for crop damage but also for taking the lives of lambs, calves, other livestock and humans.

In South America, the wild boar is also present. It is a mixture of the Russian Wild Boar and feral pigs that normally weigh between 400-600 lb. They are the result of Black Russian and European Wild Boars that had been on the Continent since the early 1900s. In Argentina, specifically, the boar has been able to overpopulate for several reasons. It is able to graze on miles of *pampas* (rich grasslands) that offer it a natural source of unlimited nourishment. Multiplication is unusually rapid as well, because the subtropical climate allows the sows to have three litters of five to ten piglets per year. Add the fact that there are no natural predators resident (even the mountain lion and jaguar are no match for a 400-lb brute), and you can begin to understand the problem Argentinean farmers have had in the 20th century.

The farmers did not use gunpowder to combat these aggressive boars or other nemeses, such as the mountain lion, jaguar and jabali. Instead, they used the *monteria criolla* style, a cultural form of hunting in Argentina, inspired by the gaucho's idea that prey should have a "fighting

chance" on the hunt, an advantage equal to that of the human hunters. This evolved from the medieval boar hunts of the European aristocracy, where large packs of dogs and mounted nobles armed with spears pursued and killed the boars. The *monteria* employs a pack of dogs that locate, chase, catch and hold the boar until the men arrive and kill the boar with a large knife. The *monteria* remains a respected tradition in Argentina. To this day, anyone that hunts wild boar with a gun is considered to be a cowardly, second-rate sportsman.

WANTED: A "SUPERDOG"

For the *monteria* to be successful, the men needed dogs suitable to the task—in fact, capable dogs were crucial not only for a successful hunt but also for one without human fatality. The dogs needed to have a great sense to locate the boar (either by air-scenting or tracking), great speed to chase the unusually quick beast, an insane amount of fearlessness to approach the boar, an inbred power to attack and overwhelm the boar and a relentless tenacity to hold the boar until the hunters arrived. In addition to all these Herculean skills, the dogs had to be fairly intelligent, trainable, focused on the hunt and able to get along with other dogs. This is quite a bit to ask of the everyday *Canis familiaris*.

Originally, the most aggressive, fastest and strongest dogs were assembled for the *monteria*. These were often crossbreeds and ideally from the lineage of the Cordoba Fighting Dog: a combination of the Mastiff, Bull Terrier and Bulldog. As you can well imagine, very few dogs could be found that were up to the task. Even the ferocious Cordoba Fighting Dog, despite its great courage and strength, was not ideally suited for *monteria*— mainly because it was nearly impossible for these dogs to work together.

ONE MAN'S MISSION

The *monteria* was a valiant and ideal style of defending the land against savage boars and other beasts. Unfortunately, without the ideal dogs, it was not a very successful endeavor. Determined to establish man's ideal partner in *monteria* was one young man by the name of Antonio Nores Martinez. In the 1920s, at the tender age of 18 years, Antonio (later Dr. Martinez) set out to create the superdog so badly needed for hunting down wild boars. He, with the help of his brother Agustin, started out with the Cordoba Fighting Dog as a base. This fearless and aggressive crossbreed had a proven record in the dog pits, where it routinely fought to the death. Such tenacity was necessary when up against a

These photos show a Dogo fighting a large boar within a controlled setting. The original purpose of the breed was to accompany Argentine farmers in the *monteria criolla* style of hunting boar.

The Great Pyrenees contributed its dense white coat and high-altitude vigor to the Dogo.

Loose lips, raw power and fearlessness were acquired from crosses to the Spanish Mastiff, a giant breed that can weigh as much as 150 lb.

400-lb pig. However, Antonio was experienced in using these dogs in hunting excursions, and knew that they would rather fight each other than chase the boar. He also wanted a dog that would be an honorable family companion and guardian, and so another breed had to be used for his self-appointed task. One by one, different breeds were added into the program as the brothers Martinez sought to achieve the ideal superdog.

Beginning with the Cordoba Fighting Dog, Antonio and Agustin developed a formula. First, to add in the Pointer, known for its keen sense of smell—the most basic element needed for tracking down the wild boar and other game. Next, the Boxer, giving both the needed vivacity and dexterity for the hunt, and the desired gentleness and docility Antonio expected of a family companion. Next, the Great Dane would be added to increase size, and the Bull Terrier to instill fearlessness, agility and aggressiveness. The old-style Bulldog (nothing like today's show dog) would add important personality traits such as boldness, obedience and tenacity, as well as physical traits, including its ample, broad chest and high-pressure jaws. The Irish Wolfhound was well known for being an instinctive hunter of wild game, and thus would make an ideal contribution. The Dogue de Bordeaux would contribute powerful, relentless jaw strength as well as good muscle structure and strength. The Great Pyrenees would be added for its vigor and dense white coat. Finally, the Spanish Mastiff would give the superdog raw power, a menacing scowl and the long, loose lips necessary for allowing breathing out the sides of the mouth while holding prey.

While attending school, the brothers began their breeding program in 1925 in Cordoba, Argentina with ten Cordoban bitches and barely enough income to keep them fed. Their father helped by hiring a kennel man to care for the dogs while the boys were in school. Family friends donated food to the dogs. First, Pointer studs were introduced until the early offspring showed promise toward the direction of Antonio's goal. Then each of the other breeds was brought in through careful steps. Antonio had a very distinct vision of what he wanted, and wrote the ideal standard for the breed in 1928. Many years passed in the painstaking program to achieve the nearly impossible goal of creating the superdog of Argentina. Tragically, Antonio did not live to see his superdog; he was killed by a thief during a boar hunt in 1956.

Younger brother Agustin took over the program, continuing to

The Great Dane's most recognizable trait—size—was added to the Dogo's lineage.

The Irish Wolfhound is famous for being an instinctive hunter of wild game and was used to contribute this hunting characteristic to the Dogo.

The Dogue de Bordeaux, the powerful French Mastiff, added jaw strength and overall muscle to the Dogo.

(Top right) The Bull Terrier is counted among the most agile of all dogs, and gladly contributed its abilities to the Dogo.

The Boxer's gentle, even temperament was used in the original Dogo recipe for success. This white Boxer puppy bears a physical resemblance to a Dogo youngster.

add new blood to the breed following the original formula and with the same conviction and precision as his brother Antonio. He moved the breeding headquarters to Esquel in Patagonia (southern Argentina), and continued to pursue his brother's dream while employed as the Argentine Ambassador to Canada. This profession turned out to be ideal for the breed, as it required overseas travel and thus provided an opportunity for Agustin to spread the Dogo Argentino throughout the world. Already the big-game hunters all over South America were using the Dogos for boar and mountain lion hunts. Soon the legend of the superdog was spreading to North America and Europe.

Finally, in 1964, the Cinologic Federation of Argentina and the Argentina Rural Society recognized the Dogo Argentino as a specific dog breed. Almost ten years later (July 31, 1973, to be exact), the Argentina Kennel Club, a member of the Fédération Cynologique Internationale (FCI), recognized the Dogo Argentino.

After gaining fame as a hunting dog in South America, the Dogo Argentino made its appearance in America.

CHARACTERISTICS OF THE
DOGO ARGENTINO

A SUPERDOG

First and foremost, the Dogo is a big-game hunter, capable of tracking prey through forests, tall grass fields and brush. But one look at this handsome white dog tells you this is no ordinary hunting dog. Exuberant musculature and powerful build give the Dogo not only great strength but also uncanny agility, speed and stamina. Considering the size of the Dogo, about 90–100 lb. when full grown, the agility of the Dogo is an amazing spectacle. One you're not likely to miss, as this breed loves to show off its athleticism.

The Dogo's speed is also impressive. Like a great sprinter, the Dogo is capable of great bursts of speed, and seems at top speed after just a few steps. The Dogo also reminds one of a thoroughbred racehorse, as he can gallop with great endurance at a fast,

steady pace.

In courage, tenacity and intelligence, the Dogo has few peers. Once focused on a subject, it is nearly impossible to get the Dogo off his goal. No rugged terrain, harsh weather or large obstacle can cause the Dogo to quit. Sometimes this singleness of purpose can be dangerous, as the Dogo rarely admits to recognizing pain and is more than willing to fight to his own death, if need be.

THE LOST CORDOBA DOG
The extinction of the original Cordoba Fighting Dog was due to the country's institution of laws banning the "sport" of dog fighting in Argentina.

If the above traits are not enough to convince one of the Dogo's versatility and athleticism, consider that this breed has seen success not only in hunting but also in obedience trials, military and police work, Schutzhund, search and rescue, and Seeing Eye® work.

TEMPERAMENT, TRAINING AND EXERCISE

The Dogo Argentino has a very strong temperament, great intelligence and, like most dogs, works very hard to please his master. This makes the breed ideal for obedience training as well as training for practical use, such as jobs around the home or farm. However, there are a few elements that must be taken into consideration when starting a training program.

First of all, do not be fooled by the cold, hard, intimidating stare that is characteristic of the breed; this look was never meant for human beings. Quite the contrary, the Dogo is a very sensitive breed that does not react well to harsh treatment from its master. Physical corrections, aside from the typical tug on a choke chain, are unnecessary and not recommended. These dogs are very receptive to positive reinforcement styles of training, and learn very quickly with this kind of handling. Use gentle, consistent corrections along with a stern

tone of voice, when necessary, and you will see rapid development.

Because the Dogo Argentino is very intelligent, he is easily bored with repetition and seemingly unnecessary tasks. To combat this, keep obedience sessions short (no more than 15 minutes) and teach the dog as many new tasks as possible. Try to mix some fun activities (like ball retrievals and flying disc games) in with his sits and stays. Your dog will sense the

Seeing is believing. A young deer suckles a Dogo bitch. This is the kind of thing that makes the patient and gentle Dogo so well loved by those who know the breed.

DOGO NUMERO UNO
The first Dogo Argentino to be shown was presented by breed founder Antonio Nores Martinez at the Hunting Dog Show, organized by the Buenos Aires Hunters Club, on September 28, 1947.

Because of the inbred hunting instinct, do not let your Dogo loose in an open field. He is likely to find prey to hunt down and may never come back. Instead, purchase a long lead like those used in tracking trials—about 36 yards in length—and get yourself in good shape so you can run with your Dogo.

THE DOGO IN THE HOME
The Dogo Argentino is a people-friendly breed and builds a long-lasting bond with his master and family. The Martinez brothers worked very carefully to instill this trait into the breed, and today the results are clearly apparent.

Talk to any Dogo owner and you will hear the same things. "She doesn't lie at my feet, she lies *on* my feet!" "He cries when we're in the next room!" "She

The Dogo makes an excellent family pet but he requires regular exercise and conditioning to maintain his magnificent, muscular body.

fun time you're having and reciprocate with like enthusiasm.

The training program you devise should give your Dogo ample exercise. Just one look at the dog's impressive musculature is enough to see that this dog is capable of great athleticism and needs activity. If you take your Dogo on hunting excursions, then you probably don't need to worry about keeping the dog active. However, if your Dogo is the family pet, then make sure you develop a vigorous exercise routine.

Ideally, the Dogo will have a lot of open space to run and roam in his domain. If this is not the case, you must bring the dog to a securely fenced area for exercise at least once or twice a week.

Dogos require a considerable area to exercise. A fenced enclosure is ideal to accommodate your Dogo.

constantly wants me to pet and hug her!" "He's like my shadow, I can't go anywhere without him following!" Indeed the Dogo longs for human contact, both physical and emotional. Although the Dogo attaches himself to his human keepers, he rarely suffers from separation anxiety. The Dogo is an ideal pet to have around children, as he will tolerate any amount of tail pulling, riding, pinching, poking or otherwise without so much as a snarl. In fact, you'd almost think the dog was enjoying the teasing that some children inflict! Make no mistake, the Dogo does not enjoy any kind of unkind treatment. Children should be instructed properly on how to handle any dog, especially one as powerful as the Dogo Argentino.

After owning a few Dogos and meeting many others, it seems

implausible that the breed is banned in some places due to its "questionable temperament." Quite the contrary, the Dogo is perhaps the most docile, abiding and sweet-hearted breed this author has ever encountered. Unfortunately, harmful breed-specific laws have banned many fabulous companion dogs from certain places. This author regrets that ignorant "dog authorities" have described the Dogo Argentino as a "giant pit bull." I have nothing derogatory to say about pit bulls, as many of these dogs are flawless companions, but it is regrettable that such a stigma is applied to the wonder dog from Argentina.

There are people who will tell you that the Dogo makes a great watchdog because he is so alert and strong, with an aggressive instinct. For the most part, this

Owning a Dogo can be an eye-opening experience. This is a tolerant and fun-loving breed that welcomes the company of humans.

Dogos adore children and will tolerate their unabashed love and handling. Proper supervision and introduction are wise whenever children and dogs are together.

If properly socialized, the Dogo can get along well with any other dog. This Japanese Shiba and Dogo Argentino are constant playmates.

may harm his master and/or loved ones.

The Dogo is not a dog to be left alone in the yard or in a kennel. Dogos gravitate to the warmth of humans and prefer to be in our company. You'll find that although the Dogo needs to be near you, he does not necessarily need constant petting and attention. He will be very happy to just lie on the floor at (more likely on) your feet and not be a nuisance.

The Dogo may become a nuisance when you leave him alone because he is a very active dog who bores very easily. Take this advice from the author, who has witnessed firsthand some beleaguering consequences of leaving the dog to entertain himself in the yard for just a few hours. One time I returned to see that the dog had found herself a "stick" to play with. In actuality this "stick" was a six-foot plank she had removed from the back deck! On another occasion I returned from a shopping trip to see that an eight-foot section of the aluminum drainpipe was missing from the side of my house. A few seconds later I spotted my precious Dogo with the pipe entrenched in her jaw, keeping her from walking through a narrow gate. Yet another time I caught the Dogo ripping the bark from the base of an old oak tree. As if fear of the dog's eating the

theory is weak. Yes, it is true that the Dogo is very alert and will investigate, out of curiosity, any unusual sounds or smells that he may sense in his area. Also, it must be understood that the Dogo was not bred to be a night watchman, but a hunter. With a hunter's instinct, it is unlikely that your Argentine superdog will be content to guard the home as his primary or only role. He is a hunter and lives for the hunt. That is not to say that the Dogo Argentino is not a guardian. In fact, because of the Dogo's strong emotional bond to his family, he will be quick to act when he perceives someone or something

house was not enough of a problem, I found that my cute overgrown puppy got moved on to digging holes the size of moon craters when she got bored with chewing on planks. At first I found these activities distressing. I was worried about what was wrong with my dog, until I spoke with other Dogo owners who had similar scary stories to tell. The lesson learned? Keep your Dogo occupied and attended and bring the dog with you whenever possible.

Along with the Dogo's bonding with man, it is also important to note that the Dogo Argentino is a one-family dog. Once bonded to his family, the Dogo will not react very well to a change in situation. If removed from his family and placed with another owner, the Dogo will suffer great anxiety and depression. Though the Dogo will eventually survive such a change, it's doubtful there will be much happiness for the animal, and the dog may show signs of stress.

All things considered, it makes sense to bring a Dogo into a loving home that intends to care for the pet for the duration of his life. This breed will get along with every person in the family and holds no special preference for a particular member. In fact, just the opposite is likely to occur; the Dogo will quickly learn the personalities and behaviors of

If you speak harshly to a Dogo, her sensitivity is obvious as her tail falls, her ears are back and she pleads for forgiveness with her eyes.

Dogos that are socialized with children from a young age behave cautiously and affectionately with them. It is vital to instruct the child about the proper way to treat a dog.

Dogos can get along well with other Dogos if properly introduced at a young age.

While we're on the subject of children, the Dogo must be socialized with children from a young age. Despite the breed's great size and strength, it is the Dogo Argentino, not the child, who is most vulnerable to injury. The Dogo is bright enough to realize that a child is very fragile, helpless and often thoughtless. In response, the Dogo will be very careful around the child and will display enormous tolerance. The child may have a tendency to take advantage of this and to do things to the dog that are harmful.

each family member, and adjust his own actions accordingly. For example, the Dogo will learn that he can take full advantage of the soft-hearted child by begging for treats, and yet will never bother imploring the stern father of the family for the same.

One obvious example that you

will likely witness is a child attempting to mount and ride the dog as if he were a horse. To the unknowing child, this is a natural assumption—after all, to a 3-foot-tall person the well-built, big Dogo may as well be a horse! But this practice must by all means be stopped immediately. Though the Dogo is broad in chest and strong in leg, he was never meant to be saddled. The child must be taught early on that the Dogo can be seriously injured by such actions because the animal is very unlikely to defend himself.

By nature, the dog will exhibit unending patience with ignorant children, partially due to his need for human attention and more so because of his high tolerance for pain. I have witnessed children try to ride, sit and lie on a Dogo; pull his tail; stretch his ears; pile items on his body; poke him with various dull and sharp objects; and stick things into the animal's eyes, ears and mouth. Through all this, the dog neither whimpers nor growls. Instead, the dog tolerates the abuse and gives a look as if to say, "Can you believe this?" To reiterate, this kind of forbearance is a characteristic of the breed, and thus it is necessary to supervise children and to instruct them on how playtime with the Dogo should proceed.

This tolerance is not always held for other animals, though it depends on the Dogo's training

and everyday purpose. The breed must be socialized with other domestic animals at an early age to curtail any possible aggression toward the family cat or rabbit. A Dogo that is trained for, and regularly used in, hunting expeditions, will most certainly be more aggressive toward other animals. Due to their innate hunting instinct, even pet Dogos that have never seen a wild boar nor participated in *monteria* will still sniff out and give chase to small rabbits and rodents that may be encountered during an outdoor excursion. This by no means identifies the Dogo Argentino as a dangerous or aggressive breed. Quite the contrary, one of the major (and realized) goals of this canine's development is to get along with other dogs in a pack for hunting purposes.

The Dogo is a self-assured, confident breed that does not look for confrontations to satisfy its insecurities. At the same time, the

Dogos deserve fair and gentle treatment from adults and children alike.

Dogo will rarely back down from a fight; but, if instigated, be aware that the Dogo will defend itself. Generally speaking, this is not a major issue. We have taken our Dogo to many parks, beaches and other public places where other dogs are present, and have had absolutely no problem. Even feisty, growling, barking dogs do not bother our superdog—she ignores them with aloofness and disinterest. She is above the challenge. Regardless of your confidence in your Dogo, keep him leashed at all times—for the sake of the breed's safety from fearful, ignorant types.

Because of the Dogo's bond to master and family, you can count on protection from the dog should you encounter an attack or some other trouble. With his strength, tenacity and intelligence, the Dogo is a guardian, who will rush in to protect you without regard to his own well-being. You can feel safe taking your Dogo for a walk down a lonely street in the middle of the night.

HEREDITARY DISEASES

As with any other large breeds of dog, the Dogo Argentino is susceptible to canine hip dysplasia (HD). When you acquire a Dogo, be sure to get hip certification papers from the breeder. If you intend to breed your Dogo, by all means have his hips x-rayed and the results sent to the Ortho-pedic Foundation for Animals (OFA). Be sure to get the dog tested and approved before breeding. Degenerative joint disease can be diagnosed on puppies four months and older; this is very important for breeders in order to rid HD from their lines. For younger puppies, breeders should provide buyers with results from diagnostic testing done on the sire and dam. Definitive clearance from HD can be ascertained when the Dogo is two years of age.

Another congenital problem to watch for is deafness. Most white-coated breeds, including Dogos, seem to have unusually high occurrences of this affliction. A dog can be deaf in only one ear (unilateral deafness) or in both (bilateral deafness). The only known hearing test for dogs is called Brainstem Auditory Evoked Response (BAER), which is usually performed on puppies eight weeks of age and older. Responsible breeders should provide BAER test results to all new Dogo owners.

Although there are no inherent eye problems apparent among Dogos, if you plan to breed be sure to screen for congenital eye disorders (such as cataracts, progressive retinal atrophy and glaucoma). Be sure to get a board-certified veterinary ophthalmologist who can issue a certificate that can be registered with CERF (Canine Eye Registry Foundation).

DO YOU KNOW ABOUT HIP DYSPLASIA?

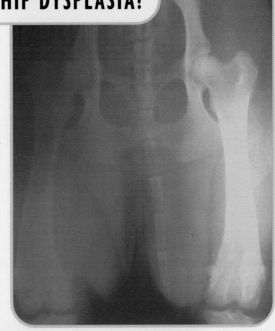

Hip dysplasia is a fairly common condition found in pure-bred dogs. When a dog has hip dysplasia, his hind leg has an incorrectly formed hip joint. By constant use of the hip joint, it becomes more and more loose, wears abnormally and may become arthritic.

Hip dysplasia can only be confirmed with an x-ray, but certain symptoms may indicate a problem. Your dog may have a hip dysplasia problem if he walks in a peculiar manner, hops instead of smoothly runs, uses his hind legs in unison (to keep the pressure off the weak joint), has trouble getting up from a prone position or always sits with both legs together on one side of his body.

As the dog matures, he may adapt well to life with a bad hip, but in a few years the arthritis develops and many dogs with hip dysplasia become crippled.

Hip dysplasia is considered an inherited disease and only can be diagnosed definitively when the dog is two years old. Some experts claim that a special diet might help your puppy outgrow the bad hip, but the usual treatments are surgical. The removal of the pectineus muscle, the removal of the round part of the femur, reconstructing the pelvis and replacing the hip with an artificial one are all surgical interventions that are expensive, but they are usually very successful. Follow the advice of your veterinarian.

X-ray of a dog with "Good" hips.

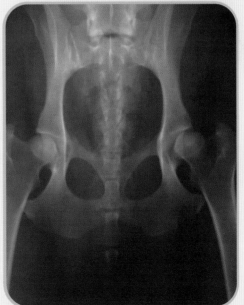

X-ray of a dog with "Moderate" dysplastic hips.

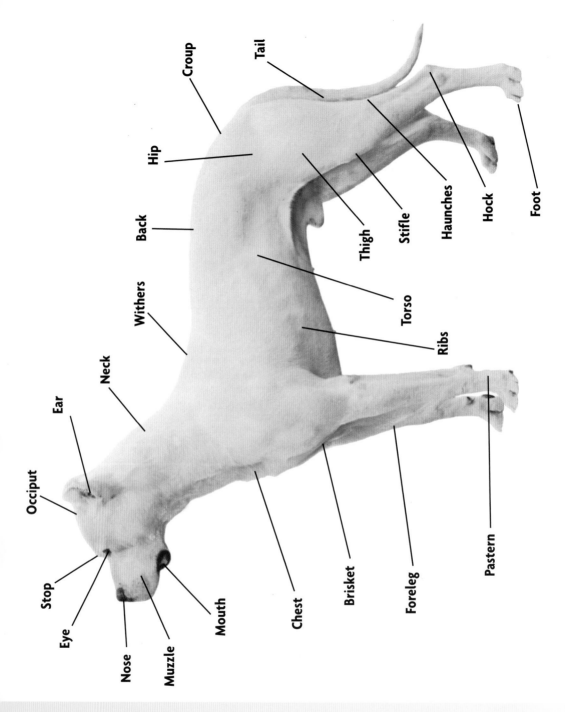

Croup

Tail

Hip

Back

Withers

Neck

Ear

Occiput

Stop

Eye

Nose

Muzzle

Mouth

Chest

Brisket

Foreleg

Pastern

Thigh

Stifle

Haunches

Hock

Foot

Torso

Ribs

Physical Structure of the Dogo Argentino

BREED STANDARD FOR THE

DOGO ARGENTINO

The breed standard for a breed is the "blueprint" for the ideal dog. The original standard for the Dogo Argentino, representing the founder's dream and intention, was published in May 1947 by Antonio Nores Martinez in *Diana* magazine (Number 89, pages 28–40, Buenos Aires, Argentina). This standard is explicit in its description of the breed, including its ideal physical type and its temperament.

Although the standard is clear, the classification of which group of dogs best suits the Dogo Argentino remains a controversial issue. Upon acceptance of El Dogo Argentino as a breed in 1964, the Argentine Canine Federation (FCA) incorporated it to its Group IX, "Hounds." Later in 1973, the Fédération Cynologique Internationale (FCI) bestowed the Dogo Argentino international recognition and placed it in Group V, "Big Game Hounds." In 1988, FCI reclassified its groups in accordance to anatomical structure, and the Dogo was transferred to Group II, "Pinscher and Schnauzer type dog, Molossoids and Swiss Mountain Dogs."

The author has chosen to include a translation of the complete standard for the Dogo Argentino in an effort to promote interest in this great breed and to preserve its true type. In America, where interest in the Dogo is very strong, breed clubs have taken the liberty to change the standard at the whim of the club officers and members. Surely, it is easier for breeders to change the standard than it is to improve the quality of their dogs! This is very bad for the Dogo. The lack of homogeneity in American-bred Dogos at shows reflects these breeders' failure to breed dogs that are morphologically and temperamentally

Although there are several Dogo Argentino standards in use today, the true standard is the original standard written by the breed's creator.

correct. The standard set forth in this text was written by the breed creator and it clearly defines what is desired in a Dogo Argentino. It is important to understand that the Dogo Argentino is a man-made breed, created by Antonio Nores Martinez, and therefore should remain "the dog he envisioned," not the dog that some wealthy influential club member happens to own. Read the standard and study it before setting out to buy a Dogo Argentino for your life.

THE OFFICIAL STANDARD FOR EL DOGO ARGENTINO

GENERAL APPEARANCE

In describing El Dogo Argentino, Antonio Nores Martinez used to say, "harmonically beautiful within the physical parameters required to perform its duty" and "…it is the only white, short-haired dog of its size and weight which are optimum to achieve its work." These statements are clearly indicative that, in this breed, form follows function; that color and size are basic identifying attributes, closely related to work performance.

Developed to find, chase and struggle with large, dangerous predators, these canines must be endowed with superior bone and muscular mass. Their large, massive head, proudly supported by a thick but graceful neck that connects to a well-balanced body, in turn supported by straight, sturdy forelegs and strong normally angulated hindquarters. The thick, long tail hangs naturally to the hocks and is carried in a smooth upwards curve. *Faults: Flaccid, overweight dogs must be severely penalized.*

The "White King of the Pampas" is a proud animal, conscious of its power, which makes it reliable and self-confident. Its striking appearance, friendly disposition, and gallant behavior have earned him this name. Females are slightly smaller than males and look distinctively feminine but without weakening substance or structure.

Judges should first consider the general appearance and overall balance of El Dogo Argentino, with utmost consideration given to type. Special attention should be afforded the head; then, to individual body components for anatomical correctness, followed by a thorough evaluation of gait efficiency.

SIZE, PROPORTION, SUBSTANCE

Height: From 23.6 to 25.6 in (60 to 65 cms), measured at the withers. **Weight**: From 88.2 to 99.2 lbs (40 to 45 kgs). **Proportion**: El Dogo Argentino is a normotype and within this class a macrotalic. Its body is slightly off-square, with body depth and length of legs, equally accounting for height.

Height and weight are important parameters subordinate to harmony and body balance which are essential to high performance. **Substance**: Heavy bones, very muscular, with a massive head, strong neck and deep-broad body. *Faults: Lean-boned, poorly muscled, slab-sided or leggy dogs to be severely penalized.*

HEAD

The head of El Dogo Argentino is one of the most typical attributes of the breed. In longitudinal section it must have a concave-convex profile. The wide, massive cranium is longitudinally and transversely convex, due to relief created by the insertion of masti-catory muscles characteristic of prey dogs. On adult specimens a

The original standard indicates that the Dogo's ears must be cropped appropriately to the size of the head. Uncropped ears are a hindrance to the hunting Dogo, being easy for prey to grab and rip.

longitudinal groove runs from muzzle to occiput. The broad, deep muzzle is slightly concave upwards, proper of dogs with great olfactory sense, capable of scenting high. Cranium and muzzle must be of equal length and join at a stop well defined but not abrupt. Occiput must be masked by the powerful neck muscles. Zygomatic arches, well separated from the skull, provide an ample cavity for comfortable insertion of the temporal muscle which, coupled with other strong masticatories, develop a positive lateral relief on cheeks and cranium. Viewed from the top, the side planes of muzzle and cranium are near parallel. The head/neck insertion must be arched and blend with the convex skull profile. Eyes are of medium size, well separated between themselves and deeply set; dark or hazelnut color, rimmed by black or flesh-colored eyelids.

Cropped ears should be short, erect or semi-erect, set high on the head, triangular in shape.

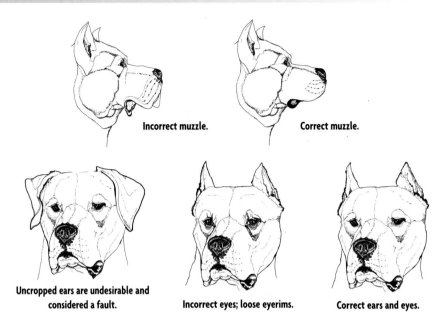

Incorrect muzzle.   Correct muzzle.

Uncropped ears are undesirable and considered a fault.   Incorrect eyes; loose eyerims.   Correct ears and eyes.

Faults: Light colored eyes or flesh-colored eyelids. Loose eyerims. Expression must be alive, intelligent and markedly hard. At attention, longitudinal wrinkles appear on the forehead. *Faults: A bland expression.* Nose is strongly pigmented in black with a slight stop at the tip and ample nostrils. Lips are closely fitting, taut, with free edges pigmented in black. A short lip is a must, to allow breathing through the back lip commissure when holding prey. Ears well on top of the head, either erect or semi-erect, of triangular shape and must always be cropped in proportion to head size. Long ears offer an easy, painful grab in the struggle with prey. Maxillaries are very strong, wide and square, functionally fitted with large, well-implanted teeth, allowing for an ample powerful bite. Without prognathism. *Faults: Narrow, rounded maxillaries to be severely penalized.* Bite in scissors is preferred; level bite is acceptable. A correct occlusion is foremost. The four large canines should close perfectly when biting to hold prey. *Faults: The lack of molars or premolars is acceptable but not desirable.*

NECK, TOPLINE, BODY
Neck stout, arched and graceful, of moderate length, proportioned to body and head size. Should present loose skin under the throat which wrinkles as in the Mastiff and freely slides over the superficial aponeurosis.

This becomes particularly useful during struggle; contender's fang or claw only injures skin, not flesh. At the same time, dog displacement inside the skin is allowed, for it to make prey. Withers very strong, of great muscular relief. Topline is highest on the withers, smoothly sloping to the croup. On adult animals, when the withers and loin muscles are well developed, the back arches down slightly. A longitudinal groove created by the relief of the dorsal muscles runs along the dog's spine. Loin is short and kidney is concealed by the dorsal muscles. Croup is muscular, round, broad and gently sloping. Tail, long and thick, tapers down to the hock joint and is set moderately high and smoothly into the croup. Carried curving smoothly upwards, naturally down at rest and always raised while struggling with prey, in continuous lateral movement, as when greeting master. Underline well muscled, with only a slight to moderate tuck-up of the abdomen. Thorax ample, on side view shall reach under the elbows. Chest ample and deep, giving impression of big lungs. Viewed from the front, the sternum must reach under the elbows. *Faults: Any deviation from characteristics described herein, to be severely penalized.*

FOREQUARTERS
Forelegs are straight, thick and vertical; set wide apart. *Faults: Long or thin forelegs. Narrow or fiddle front. Toeing or rolling (in or out).* Shoulders tight, muscular and powerful. Shoulder blades of equal length and at right angle with humerus. *Faults: Incorrect angulation.* Elbows parallel to the body. *Faults: In or out elbows.* The pastern strong and near vertical. *Faults: Knuckled over or down in pasterns.* Feet are round and compact with short, tight, close-together toes, proportioned to paw size. Toes and paws having fleshy, rough pads of dark color. Nails short, strong, and white. *Faults: Disproportionate, hare, flat or splay feet.*

HINDQUARTERS
Broad, with very muscular thighs and short rear pasterns. Normally angulated. Hind legs well apart and parallel. Strong hocks, perpendicular to the ground, neither turned in or out. Rear feet similar to front feet but slightly smaller. Without dewclaws. *Faults: Any deviation from characteristics described herein, to be severely penalized.*

COAT
Short and thick with a glossy sheen. Hair is stiff, coarse and of uniform length. A field conditioned coat or working scars should never be faulted. *Faults: Long or wavy coat. Thin hair.*

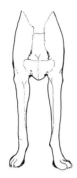

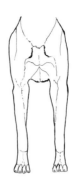

Incorrect forequarters; narrow chest, light boned.

Incorrect forequarters; lack of depth of chest.

Correct forequarters.

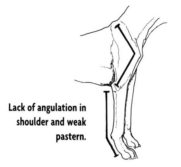

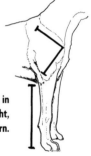

Lack of angulation in shoulder and weak pastern.

Proper angulation in shoulder and straight, strong pastern.

COLOR

Completely white.

GAIT

A superb canine athlete, the massively muscled Dogo Argentino, when in motion, is a larger than life combination of barely contained explosive power and lightning speed, coupled with tremendous stamina and unbelievable agility. Viewed from the side, the powerful, smooth and effortless trot is produced by a long, sleek front reach, balanced with an immensely powerful rear drive. The topline is held level and firm. Viewed from the front or rear, the legs are parallel but converge toward centerline as speed increases. The front and rear legs remain in a straight column of support, and legs on the same side move in the same plane. At a walk, he moves like a lion; with power, dignity and the supreme confidence that he is king of all he surveys. *Faults: In*

order to function as a boar hunter or working dog, soundness is paramount. It is critical that these animals move powerfully, swiftly and effortlessly; therefore, any wobbling, twisting, choppiness, interference or other deviation that decreases power, speed or efficiency be severely penalized.

TEMPERAMENT

A magnificent hunter of wild boar and mountain lion. El Dogo Argentino has extremely strong hunting instincts, incredible determination and legendary courage. Very alert and jovial, he possesses uncanny intelligence and a keen wit. This is a very people-oriented dog, who is extremely friendly and outgoing, unless given reason to be otherwise. His self-confidence makes him very trusting of humans with whom he is patient and communicative. While being incredibly obedient and willing to please, he is extremely sensitive to his handler and cannot tolerate forceful training methods. This versatile animal is capable of intense concentration, learns rapidly and retains what is learned almost indefinitely; however, he is easily bored by overwork and repetition. A good watchdog, El Dogo Argentino is calm around the house, yet he is alert and ready at a moment's notice; however, this is not his primary function—he is a hunter, first and foremost. As such, he is not a barking dog, although he is endowed with a thunderous bark, modulated rhythmic and constant when he

The Dogo is a strong, active dog that exhibits great agility in running, climbing and jumping.

The Dogo can be as gentle and loving with children as he is fearless and powerful when hunting boars and mountain lions.

wants to call attention to something he deems important. He is a one-family dog who needs close contact with all members and is unhappy when separated from them. When properly socialized with children, he is notably tolerant and gentle. He should also be socialized with domestic animals at an early age, to curtail any subsequent aggression towards them. Males and females are very stable and remarkably sweet while being tough to the core. They are more like a force of Nature than a mere animal. *Faults: Sluggishness, lack of intelligence, aloofness. Any hint of shyness or unprovoked aggression must be severely penalized.*

REASON FOR DISQUALIFICATION
Lack of type. Height below 23.6 in (60 cms). Any physical disproportion. Atypical heads. Dissimilarly colored eyes. Walleyes. Flesh-colored and predominantly flesh-colored nose. Split nose. Harelip. Overly pendulous lip. Uncropped ears. Deafness (either bilateral or unilateral). Overbite. Underbite. All spots of color.

This litter of Dogos has many lovely solid-white puppies that may be very promising, typical Dogos. The puppy with the spot of color over his eye would be disqualified from competing in the show ring.

The ideal Dogo appears attentive, intelligent and alert. These characteristics make the breed suitable for many tasks, including guarding, hunting and police work.

DOGO ARGENTINO

BEFORE YOU BUY A DOGO

The foremost need for owning a Dogo Argentino is commitment. You and your family must be willing to provide a stable, loving home for the duration of the animal's life—usually at least ten years. You also must be willing to furnish the space a Dogo needs to exercise. You need not live on a 10-acre farm but at least be able to bring the dog somewhere nearby where he can run hard and long on a regular basis. The Dogo is not high-strung, but he is athletic and needs to expend energy.

Though your Dogo needs to run, do not let him roam free. This breed is made for hunting and will follow its all-knowing nose—not necessarily your commands. Because of his hunting instinct, it is vital to teach at least basic obedience (sit, stay, come), as this may one day save the dog's life.

If you have livestock or other pets around the house, consider getting a female Dogo. She will be less likely to be aggressively dominant in the home.

While Dogos enjoy the warm sun, they are not as intolerant of the cold as you might expect, given their short coats. Dogos kept in Esquel, Chubut (Argentina) by Agustin Nores Martinez did quite well in colder climes (approximately 42 degrees latitude).

Be prepared to give loads of attention and, at the same time, be capable of ruling with an iron fist, if need be. These are very strong-willed and physically powerful dogs with the added element of wit and charm. As sweet as they are, they are equally bright and manipulative, and will turn weak-minded people into their puppets.

Finally, expect to pay a high price for a well-bred Dogo; after all, this is a superdog! "You get

INHERIT THE MIND

In order to know whether or not a puppy will fit into your lifestyle, you need to assess his personality. A good way to do this is to interact with his parents. Your pup inherits not only his appearance but also his personality and temperament from the sire and dam. If the parents are fearful or overly aggressive, these same traits may likely show up in your puppy.

what you pay for" is an expression that particularly applies to the purchase of a dog. If someone is offering a Dogo at the same price as you might pay for a dog as common as a pet Labrador Retriever, do some more investigation into the breeder's background. These dogs are rare and thus command a high price.

OWNER CONSIDERATIONS

Although the reader of these pages is more likely interested in finding a companionable, family animal than a show champion or hunting dog, there remain many serious factors governing your choice. A primary consideration is time, not only the time of the animal's allotted lifespan, which is about ten years, but also the time required for the owner to exercise and care for the creature. If you are not committed to the welfare and whole existence of this energetic, purposeful animal; if, in the simplest, most basic example, you are not willing to walk your dog daily, despite the weather, do not choose a Dogo Argentino.

Space is another important consideration. The Dogo Argentino in early puppyhood may be well accommodated in a corner of your kitchen, but after only four months, a larger space certainly will be demanded. A yard with a reliable fence is also

ARE YOU PREPARED?
Unfortunately, when a puppy is bought by someone who does not take into consideration the time and attention that dog ownership requires, it is the puppy who suffers when he is either abandoned or placed in a shelter by a frustrated owner. So all of the "homework" you do in preparation for your pup's arrival will benefit you both. The more informed you are, the more you will know what to expect and the better equipped you will be to handle the ups and downs of raising a puppy. Hopefully, everyone in the household is willing to do his part in raising and caring for the pup. The anticipation of owning a dog often brings a lot of promises from excited family members: "I will walk him every day," "I will feed him," "I will house-train him," etc., but these things take time and effort, and promises can easily be forgotten once the novelty of the new pet has worn off.

a basic and reasonable expectation.

There are also the usual problems associated with puppies of any breed like the damage likely to be sustained by your floors, furniture and landscape. Your freedom of movement and ease in taking vacations or weekend trips will also be affected. This union is a serious affair and should be thoughtfully considered but once decided, be assured that a Dogo Argentino is, perhaps, the most rewarding of all breeds.

WHERE TO BEGIN?
If you are convinced that the Dogo Argentino is the ideal dog for you,

Selecting a breeder of Dogos requires some research, and the potential owner must be patient and well informed. Your goal must be to find a typical, temperamentally fit Dogo.

it's time to learn about where to find a puppy and what to look for. No matter what breed of dog you're seeking, finding a good breeder takes time, patience and persistence. Dogo Argentino is a rare breed and finding a qualified Dogo Argentino breeder can be a difficult process. Start by contacting a breed club or rare-breed-dog club. Today's technology offers the power of the Internet and you can find a number of breeders advertising themselves there.

Because the Dogo is rather uncommon, it's extremely important for you to have a thorough understanding of the breed. Study the breed standard, and re-study the finer details over and over until you believe you truly know the breed. Try, if you can, to visit a dog show or match that will have Dogos involved and compare what you've studied to what you see. Meet the breeders and handlers firsthand and get an idea what Dogo Argentinos look like outside a photographer's lens. Provided you approach the handlers when they are not terribly busy with the dogs, most are more than willing to answer questions, recommend breeders and give advice.

You should seek out as many breeders as possible, and talk to them about their experience with the breed. For the most part, true Dogo breeders are walking historians of the breed and very sensi-

TEMPERAMENT COUNTS

Your selection of a good puppy can be determined by your needs. A show potential or a good pet? It is your choice. Every puppy, however, should be of good temperament. Although show-quality puppies are bred and raised with emphasis on physical conformation, responsible breeders strive for equally good temperament. Do not buy from a breeder who concentrates solely on physical beauty at the expense of personality.

tive to preserving the image that Antonio and Augustin Nores Martinez worked so hard to create. Be wary of any breeders that are quick to tend to your every whim, and avoid any breeders that don't ask you any questions. For the most part, the typical Dogo Argentino breeder is more concerned with the home his offspring is getting than anything else.

A reputable breeder is the

safest method of obtaining your puppy. This is recommended even if you are not looking for a show specimen. Look for an established breeder with outstanding dog ethics and a strong commitment to the breed. New owners should have as many questions as they have doubts. An established breeder is indeed the one to answer your four million questions and make you comfortable with your choice of the Dogo Argentino. An established breeder will sell you a puppy at a fair price if, and only if, the breeder determines that you are a suitable, worthy owner of his dogs. An established breeder can be relied upon for advice, no matter what time of day or night. A reputable breeder will accept a puppy back, without questions, should you decide that this is not the right dog for you.

When choosing a breeder, reputation is much more important than convenience of location. Do not be overly impressed by breeders who run brag advertisements in the presses about their stupendous champions and hunting lines. The real quality breeders are quiet and unassuming. You will hear about the true Dogo breeders at dog shows—they are usually the breeders behind the dogs taking home the Best of Breed awards.

While health considerations in the Dogo Argentino are not nearly as daunting as in most other breeds, socialization is a breeder concern of immense importance. Since the Dogo Argentino's temperament can vary from line to line, socialization is the first and best way to encourage a proper, stable personality.

Once you have contacted and met a breeder or two and made your choice about which breeder is best suited to your needs, it's time to visit the litter. Keep in mind that many top breeders have waiting lists. Sometimes new owners have to wait as long as

PUPPY APPEARANCE

Your puppy should have a well-fed appearance but not a distended abdomen, which may indicate worms or incorrect feeding, or both. The body should be firm, with a solid feel. The skin of the abdomen should be pale pink and clean, without signs of scratching or rash. Check the hind legs to make certain that dewclaws were removed, if any were present at birth.

There are other subtle differences between the sexes. As might be expected, females are generally more affectionate than males. The female thoroughly enjoys constant petting, massaging and hugging—she craves cuddling and snuggling. Interestingly enough, this trait has no effect whatsoever on

Select the puppy that is outgoing and appealing. A mutual attraction can only add to the love affair with your new dog.

two years for a puppy. If you are really committed to the breeder whom you've selected, then you will wait (and hope for an early arrival or cancellation!). Don't be too anxious, however. If your second-choice breeder doesn't have a waiting list, or any puppy buyers, there is probably a reason.

The gender of your puppy is largely a matter of personal taste, although there is a common belief among those who work with Dogo Argentinos that bitches are quicker to learn and less aggressive. Males learn more slowly but retain the lesson longer. Male dogs are equally devoted and loyal but have the drawback of being in season all year and, therefore, prone to possible wandering.

PEDIGREE VS. REGISTRATION CERTIFICATE

Too often new owners are confused between these two important documents. Your puppy's pedigree, essentially a family tree, is a written record of a dog's genealogy of three generations or more. The pedigree will show you the names as well as performance titles of all dogs in your pup's background. Your breeder must provide you with a registration application, with his part properly filled out. You must complete the application and send it to the registry with the proper fee. Every puppy must come from a litter that has been registered by the breeder, born in the USA and from a sire and dam that are also registered with the kennel club.

The seller must provide you with complete records to identify the puppy. The registry may require that the seller provide the buyer with the following: breed; sex; date of birth; litter number (when available); names and registration numbers of the parents; breeder's name; and date sold or delivered.

the females' hunting ability. In Argentina, there are just as many female Dogos heading the *monteria*, and they are just as willing to attack and fight to the death. Supposedly, the females have slightly sharper senses and hunting instincts—or at least this is what many hunters claim. Perhaps the fact that females are more apt to follow the directions of the master (except when in heat!) and are more focused on the hunt makes them appear to have stronger instincts.

Adult males will not be as physically needy but are still more affectionate than most big breeds. They also are very outgoing and friendly with people properly introduced to them. During the daily routine, however,

> **YOUR SCHEDULE . . .**
> If you lead an erratic, unpredictable life, with daily or weekly changes in your work requirements, consider the problems of owning a puppy. The new puppy has to be fed regularly, socialized (loved, petted, handled, introduced to other people) and, most importantly, allowed to go outdoors for house-training. As the dog gets older, he can be more tolerant of deviations in his feeding and relief schedule.

the males tend to be independent and even arrogant toward the other members of the family, often retreating to a quiet, sunlit room in a remote corner of the house.

Generally speaking, the males are more likely to challenge the master's dominance, and thus need an experienced, mentally tough dog owner. Females are not quite as dominant and are the better choice if children are in the family. However, be sure to keep a very tight grip on a very short leash when the female Dogo is in heat. She will take any chance available to burst from restraint if she thinks there is a male dog within a 10-mile radius.

Your Dogo Argentino's coat must be completely white. Any marking or spot of any color is considered an atavistic characteristic. Your puppy should have a dark nose and eyes. These are a

Daily exercise and companionship are just two of the things you need to provide for your Dogo.

consideration of pigmentation, which should not be confused with color. Look for expression in your puppy's eyes, as this is a good sign of intelligence.

Note the way your choice moves. The Dogo Argentino, even in puppyhood, should show light and swift movement with no tendency to stumble or drag the hind feet. Look at the mouth to make sure that the bite is fairly even, although maturity can often correct errors present at puppyhood. If you have any doubts, ask to see the parents' mouths. This brings up an important point—do not buy a puppy without first seeing at least one of the parents.

Breeders commonly allow visitors to see the litter by around the fifth or sixth week, and puppies leave for their new homes between the eighth and tenth week. Breeders who permit their puppies to leave early are more interested in your money than their puppies' well-being. Puppies need to learn the rules of the trade from their dam, and most dams continue teaching the pups manners and dos and don'ts until around the eighth week. Breeders spend significant amounts of time with the Dogo Argentino toddlers so that they are able to interact with the "other species," i.e., humans. Given the long history that dogs and humans have, bonding between the two species is natural but

PET INSURANCE

Just as you can insure your car, your house and your own health, you likewise can insure your dog's health. Investigate a pet insurance policy by talking to your vet. Depending on the age of your dog, the breed and the kind of coverage you desire, your policy can be very affordable. Most policies cover accidental injuries, poisoning and thousands of medical problems and illnesses, including cancers. Some carriers also offer routine care and immunization coverage.

must be nurtured. A well-bred, well-socialized Dogo Argentino pup wants nothing more than to be near you and to please you.

COMMITMENT OF OWNERSHIP
After considering all of these factors, you have most likely already made some very important decisions about selecting

your puppy. You have chosen a Dogo Argentino, which means that you have decided which characteristics you want in a dog and what type of dog will best fit into your family and lifestyle. If you have selected a breeder, you have gone a step further—you have done your research and found a responsible, conscientious person who breeds quality Dogo Argentinos and who should be a reliable source of help as you and your puppy adjust to life together. If you have observed a litter in action, you have obtained a firsthand look at the dynamics of a puppy "pack" and, thus, you have learned about each pup's individual personality—perhaps you have even found one that particularly appeals to you.

However, even if you have not yet found the Dogo Argentino puppy of your dreams, observing pups will help you learn to recognize certain behavior and to determine what a pup's behavior indicates about his temperament. You will be able to pick out which pups are the leaders, which ones are less outgoing, which ones are confident, which ones are shy, playful, friendly, aggressive, etc. Equally as important, you will learn to recognize what a healthy pup should look and act like. All of these things will help you in your search, and when you find the Dogo Argentino that was meant for you, you will know it!

Researching your breed, selecting a responsible breeder and observing as many pups as possible are all important steps on the way to dog ownership. It may seem like a lot of effort...and you have not even brought the pup home yet! Remember, though, you cannot be too careful when it comes to deciding on the type of dog you want and finding out about your prospective pup's background. Buying a puppy is not—or should not be—just another whimsical purchase. This is one instance in which you actually do get to choose your own family! You may be thinking that

Puppies quickly bond with their new owners, and by three months of age want nothing more than to be near you and to please you.

buying a puppy should be fun—it should not be so serious and so much work. Keep in mind that your puppy will become a real member of your family. You will come to realize that, while buying a puppy is a pleasurable and exciting endeavor, it is not something to be taken lightly. Relax... the fun will start when the pup comes home!

Always keep in mind that a puppy is nothing more than a baby in a furry disguise...a baby who is virtually helpless in a human world and who trusts his owner for fulfillment of his basic needs for survival. In addition to food, water and shelter, your pup needs care, protection, guidance and love. If you are not prepared to commit to this, then you are not prepared to own a dog.

PREPARING PUPPY'S PLACE IN YOUR HOME

Researching your breed and finding a breeder are only two aspects of the "homework" you will have to do before bringing your Dogo Argentino puppy home. You will also have to prepare your home and family for the new addition. Much as you would prepare a nursery for a newborn baby, you will need to designate a place in your home that will be the puppy's own. How you prepare your home will depend on how much freedom the dog will be allowed. Will he be confined to

QUALITY FOOD
The cost of food must be mentioned. All dogs need a good-quality food with an adequate supply of protein to develop their bones and muscles properly. Most dogs are not picky eaters but, unless fed properly, can quickly succumb to skin problems.

one room or a specific area in the house, or will he be allowed to roam as he pleases? Whatever you decide, you must ensure that he has a place that he can "call his own."

When you bring your new puppy into your home, you are bringing him into what will become his home as well. Obviously, you did not buy a puppy so that he could take over your house, but in order for a puppy to grow into a stable, well-adjusted dog, he has to feel comfortable in his surroundings. Remember, he is leaving the warmth and security of his dam and littermates, as well as the familiarity of the only place he has ever known, so it is important to make his transition as easy

PHOTO COURTESY OF DOSKOCIL

Your local pet shop should have a wide variety of crates from which you can choose.

your puppy must be feeling. It is up to you to reassure him and to let him know, "Little *perro*, you are going to like it here!"

WHAT YOU SHOULD BUY

CRATE

To someone unfamiliar with the use of crates in dog training, it may seem like punishment to shut a dog in a crate, but this is not the case at all. Most breeders and trainers are recommending the crate as a preferred tool for pet puppies as well as show puppies. Crates are not cruel—crates have many humane and highly effective uses in dog care and training. For example, crate training is a very popular and very successful housebreaking method. A crate can keep your dog safe during travel; and, perhaps most importantly, a crate provides your dog with a place of his own in your home. It serves as a "doggie bedroom" of sorts—your Dogo Argentino can curl up in his crate when he wants to sleep or when he just needs a break. Many dogs sleep in their crates overnight. With soft bedding and a favorite chew toy placed inside, a crate becomes a cozy pseudo-den for your dog. Like his ancestors, he too will seek out the comfort and retreat of a den—you just happen to be providing him with something a little more luxurious than his early ancestors enjoyed.

as possible. By preparing a place in your home for the puppy, you are making him feel as welcome as possible in a strange new place. It should not take him long to get used to it, but the sudden shock of being transplanted is somewhat traumatic for a young pup. Imagine how a small child would feel in the same situation—that is how

CRATE-TRAINING TIPS

During crate training, you should partition off the section of the crate in which the pup stays. If he is given too big an area, this will hinder your training efforts. Crate training is based on the fact that a dog does not like to soil his sleeping quarters, so it is ineffective to keep a pup in an area that is so big that he can eliminate in one end and get far enough away from it to sleep. Also, you want to make the crate den-like for the pup. Blankets and a favorite toy will make the crate cozy for the small pup; as he grows, you may want to evict some of his "roommates" to make more room. It will take some coaxing at first, but be patient. Given some time to get used to it, your pup will adapt to his new home-within-a-home quite nicely.

As far as purchasing a crate, the type that you buy is up to you. It will most likely be one of the two most popular types: wire or fiberglass. There are advantages and disadvantages to each type. For example, a wire crate is more open, allowing the air to flow through and affording the dog a view of what is going on around him, while a fiberglass crate is sturdier. Both can double as travel crates, providing protection for the dog. The size of the crate is another thing to consider. Puppies do not stay puppies forever—in fact, sometimes it seems as if they grow right before your eyes. A mid-sized crate may be fine for a very young Dogo Argentino pup, but it will not do him much good for long! Unless you have the money and the inclination to buy a new crate every time your pup has a growth spurt, it is better to get one that will accommodate your dog both as a pup and at full size. A large-size crate will be necessary for a full-grown Dogo Argentino, who stands approximately 25 inches high.

BEDDING

A soft crate pad in the dog's crate will help the dog feel more at home, and you may wish to offer him a small blanket. First, the bedding will take the place of the leaves, twigs, etc., that the pup would use in the wild to make a den; the pup can make his own

This Dogo puppy is not only crate trained but also acclimated to various domestic animals as well. He doesn't seem to mind a visit from his ferret friend.

Your local pet shop will almost surely have a complete supply of crates from which you can make your selection. Buy a crate large enough to accommodate your Dogo when he becomes an adult.

Most dogs that have been crate trained would rather rest in a crate than anywhere else. By all means, crate train your Dogo puppy.

"burrow" in the crate. Although your pup is far removed from his den-making ancestors, the denning instinct is still a part of his genetic makeup. Second, until you bring your pup home, he has been sleeping amid the warmth of his dam and littermates, and while a blanket is not the same as a warm, breathing body, it still provides heat and something with which to snuggle. You will want to wash your pup's bedding frequently in case he has an accident in his crate, and replace or remove any blanket that becomes ragged and starts to fall apart.

Toys

Toys are a must for dogs of all ages, especially for curious playful pups. Puppies are the "children" of the dog world, and what child does not love toys? Chew toys provide enjoyment to both dog and owner—your dog will enjoy playing with his favorite toys, while you will enjoy the fact that they distract him from your expensive shoes and leather sofa. Puppies love to chew; in fact,

MENTAL AND DENTAL

Toys not only help your puppy get the physical and mental stimulation he needs but also provide a great way to keep his teeth clean. Hard rubber or nylon toys, especially those constructed with grooves, are designed to scrape away plaque, preventing bad breath and gum infection.

chewing is a physical need for pups as they are teething, and everything looks appetizing! The full range of your possessions—from new sneakers to Oriental carpet—are fair game in the eyes of a teething pup. Puppies are not all that discerning when it comes to finding something to literally "sink their teeth into"—everything tastes great!

Dogo Argentino puppies are very aggressive chewers and only the hardest, strongest toys should be offered to them. Breeders advise owners to resist stuffed toys because they can become de-stuffed in no time. The overly excited pup may ingest the stuffing, which is neither digestible nor nutritious.

Similarly, squeaky toys are quite popular, but must be avoided for the Dogo Argentino. Perhaps a squeaky toy can be used as an aid in training, but not for free play. If a pup "disembowels" one of these, the small plastic squeaker inside can be dangerous if swallowed. Monitor the condition of all your pup's toys carefully and get rid of any that have been chewed to the point of becoming potentially dangerous.

Be careful of natural bones, which have a tendency to splinter into sharp, dangerous pieces. Also be careful of rawhide, which can turn into pieces that are easy to swallow or into a mushy mess on your carpet.

LEAD

A nylon lead is probably the best option as it is the most resistant to puppy teeth should your pup take a liking to chewing on his lead. Of course, this is a habit that should be nipped in the bud, but if your pup likes to chew on his lead he has a very slim chance of being able to chew

TOYS, TOYS, TOYS!

With a big variety of dog toys available, and so many that look like they would be a lot of fun for a dog, be careful in your selection. It is amazing what a set of puppy teeth can do to an innocent-looking toy, so, obviously, safety is a major consideration. Be sure to choose the most durable products that you can find. Hard nylon bones and toys are a safe bet, and many of them are offered in different scents and flavors that will be sure to capture your dog's attention. It is always fun to play a game of fetch with your dog, and there are balls and flying discs that are specially made to withstand dog teeth.

FINANCIAL RESPONSIBILITY

Grooming tools, collars, leashes, crate, dog beds and, of course, toys will be expenses to you when you first obtain your pup, and the cost will continue throughout your dog's lifetime. If your puppy damages or destroys your possessions (as most puppies surely will!) or something belonging to a neighbor, you can calculate additional expense. There is also flea and pest control, which every dog owner faces more than once. You must be able to handle the financial responsibility of owning a dog.

up, you will need to purchase a stronger leather or chain lead to control your Dogo. Of course there are special leads for training purposes, and specially made leather harnesses for working Dogo Argentinos, but these are not necessary for routine walks.

COLLAR

Your pup should get used to wearing a collar all the time since you will want to attach his ID tags to it. A lightweight nylon collar is a good choice; make sure that it fits snugly enough so that the pup cannot wriggle out of it, but is loose enough so that it will not be uncomfortably tight around the pup's neck. You should be able to fit a finger between the pup and the collar. It may take some time for your pup to get used to wearing the collar, but soon he will not even notice that it is there. Choke collars are made for training, and you should learn how to use one properly before putting it on your Dogo.

FOOD AND WATER BOWLS

Your pup will need two bowls, one for food and one for water. You may want two sets of bowls, one for inside and one for outside, depending on where the dog will be fed and where he will be spending most of his time. Stainless steel or sturdy plastic bowls are popular choices. Plastic bowls are more chewable. Dogs tend not

through the strong nylon. Nylon leads are also lightweight, which is good for a young Dogo Argentino who is just getting used to the idea of walking on a lead. For everyday walking and safety purposes, the nylon lead is a good choice. As your pup grows

The BUCKLE COLLAR is the standard collar used for everyday purposes. Be sure that you adjust the buckle on growing puppies. Check it every day. It can become too tight overnight! These collars can be made of leather or nylon. Attach your dog's identification tags to this collar.

The CHOKE COLLAR is the usual collar recommended for training. It is constructed of highly polished steel so that it slides easily through the stainless steel loop. The idea is that the dog controls the pressure around his neck and he will stop pulling if the collar becomes uncomfortable. Never leave a choke collar on your dog when not training.

The HALTER is for a trained dog that has to be restrained to prevent running away, chasing a cat and the like. Considered the most humane of all collars, it is frequently used on smaller dogs for which collars are not comfortable.

Provide your Dogo with feeding and watering bowls. These bowls can be constructed of sturdy plastic, ceramic, clay or stainless steel.

to chew on the steel variety, which can be sterilized. It is important to buy sturdy bowls since anything is in danger of being chewed by puppy teeth and you do not want your dog to be constantly chewing apart his bowl (for his safety and for your wallet!).

CLEANING SUPPLIES

Until a pup is house-trained, you will be doing a lot of cleaning. Accidents will occur, which is okay in the beginning because the puppy does not know any better. All you can do is be prepared to clean up any accidents. Old rags, towels, newspapers and a safe disinfectant are good to have on hand.

BEYOND THE BASICS

The items previously discussed are the bare necessities. You will find out what else you need as you go along—grooming supplies, flea/tick protection, baby gates to partition a room, etc. These things will vary depending on your situ-

A sturdy collar is best used for training your Dogo. The lead and collar should be made of a strong material.

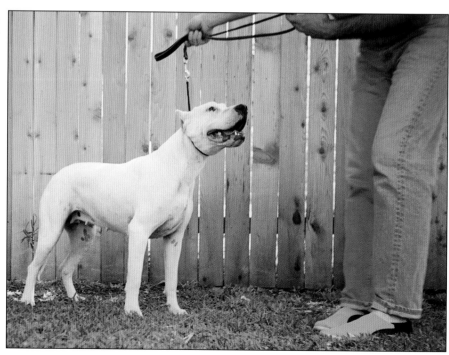

ation but it is important that you have everything you need to feed and make your Dogo Argentino comfortable in his first few days at home.

PUPPY-PROOFING YOUR HOME

Aside from making sure that your Dogo Argentino will be comfortable in your home, you also have to make sure that your home is safe for your Dogo Argentino. This means taking precautions that your pup will not get into anything he should not get into and that there is nothing within his reach that may harm him should he sniff it, chew it, inspect it, etc. This probably seems obvious since, while you are primarily concerned with your pup's safety, at the same time you do not want

Your local pet shop sells an array of dishes and bowls for water and food.

It is your responsibility to clean up after your dog has relieved himself. Pet shops have various aids to assist in the cleanup job.

NATURAL TOXINS

Examine your grass and landscaping before bringing your puppy home. Many varieties of plants have leaves, stems or flowers that are toxic if ingested, and you can depend on a curious puppy to investigate them. Ask your vet for information on poisonous plants or research them at your library.

If you see your dog carrying a piece of vegetation in his mouth, approach him in a quiet, disinterested manner, avoid eye contact, pet him and gradually remove the plant from his mouth. Alternatively, offer him a treat and maybe he'll drop the plant on his own accord. Be sure no toxic plants are growing in your own yard or kept in your home.

the house, keep any potentially dangerous items in the "off-limits" areas. An electrical cord can pose a danger should the puppy decide to taste it—and who is going to convince a pup that it would not make a great chew toy? Cords should be fastened tightly against the wall. If your dog is going to spend time in a crate, make sure that there is nothing near his crate that he can reach if he sticks his curious little nose or paws through the openings. Just as you would with a child, keep all household cleaners and chemicals where the pup cannot get to them.

It is also important to make sure that the outside of your home is safe. Of course your puppy should never be unsupervised, but a pup let loose in the yard will want to run and explore, and he should be granted that freedom. Do not let a fence give you a false sense of security; you would be surprised how crafty (and persistent) a dog can be in figuring out how to dig under and squeeze his way through small holes, or to jump or climb over a fence. The remedy is to make the fence high enough so that it really is impossible for your dog to get over it (about 8 feet should suffice), and well embedded into the ground. Be sure to repair or secure any gaps in the fence. Check the fence periodically to ensure that it is in good shape and make repairs as

your belongings to be ruined. Breakables should be placed out of reach if your dog is to have full run of the house. If he is to be limited to certain places within

needed; a very determined pup may return to the same spot to "work on it" until he is able to get through. Dogos are devoted diggers—so be forewarned!

FIRST TRIP TO THE VET
You have picked out your puppy, and your home and family are ready. Now all you have to do is collect your Dogo Argentino from the breeder and the fun begins, right? Well…not so fast. Something else you need to prepare is your pup's first trip to the veterinarian. Perhaps the breeder can recommend someone in the area who specializes in large-breed dogs, or maybe you know some other Dogo

SKULL & CROSSBONES
Thoroughly puppy-proof your house before bringing your puppy home. Never use cockroach or rodent poisons or plant fertilizers in any area accessible to the puppy. Avoid the use of toilet cleaners. Most dogs are born with "toilet-bowl sonar" and will take a drink if the lid is left open. Also keep the trash secured and out of reach.

Nothing is more important than making your Dogo comfortable in your home and socialized with all members of the family.

Argentino owners who can suggest a good vet. Either way, you should have an appointment arranged for your pup before you pick him up and schedule an examination before taking him home.

The pup's first visit will consist of an overall examination to make sure that the pup does not have any problems that are not apparent to you. The veterinarian will also set up a schedule for the pup's vaccinations; the breeder will inform you of which ones the pup has already received and the vet can continue from there.

INTRODUCTION TO THE FAMILY

Everyone in the house will be excited about the puppy's coming home and will want to pet him and play with him, but it is best to make the introductions low-key so as not to overwhelm the puppy. He is apprehensive already. It is

Be sure there are no potentially toxic plants growing in your own backyard.

> **THE RIDE HOME**
> Taking your dog from the breeder to your home in a car can be a very uncomfortable experience for both of you. The puppy will have been taken from his warm, friendly, safe environment and brought into a strange new environment—an environment that moves! Be prepared for loose bowels, urination, crying, whining and even fear biting. With proper love and encouragement when you arrive home, the stress of the trip should quickly disappear.

the first time he has been separated from his dam and the breeder, and the ride to your home is likely the first time he has been in a car. The last thing you want to do is smother him, as this will only frighten him further. This is not to say that human contact is not extremely necessary at this stage, because this is the time when a connection between the pup and his human family is formed. Gentle petting and soothing words should help console him, as well as just putting him down and letting him explore on his own (under your watchful eye, of course).

The pup may approach the family members or may busy himself with exploring for a while. Gradually, each person should spend some time with the pup, one at a time, crouching down to get as close to the pup's level as possible and letting him sniff their hands and petting him gently. He definitely needs human attention and he needs to be touched—this is how to form an immediate bond. Just remember that the pup is experiencing a lot of things for the first time, at the same time. There are new people, new noises, new smells and new things to investigate: so be gentle, be affectionate and be as comforting as you can be.

YOUR PUP'S FIRST NIGHT HOME

You have traveled home with your new charge safely in his crate. He's been to the vet for a thorough checkup; he's been weighed, his papers examined; perhaps he's even been vaccinated and wormed as well. He's met the

family, licked the whole family, including the excited children and the less-than-happy cat. He's explored his area, his new bed, the yard and anywhere else he's been permitted. He's eaten his first meal at home and relieved himself in the proper place. He's heard lots of new sounds, smelled new friends and seen more of the outside world than ever before.

That was just the first day! He's worn out and is ready for bed…or so you think!

It's puppy's first night and you are ready to say "Good night"— keep in mind that this is puppy's first night ever to be sleeping alone. His dam and littermates are no longer at paw's length and he's a bit scared, cold and lonely. Be reassuring to your new family member. This is not the time to spoil him and give in to his inevitable whining.

Puppies whine. They whine to let the others know where they

Follow your nose! The Dogo is a hunter, always searching for prey. Keep your Dogo on a leash whenever in a strange place.

ELECTRICAL FENCING

The electrical fencing system which forms an invisible fence works on a battery-operated collar that shocks the dog if it gets too close to the buried (or elevated) wire. There are some people who think very highly of this system of controlling a dog's wandering. Keep in mind that the collar has batteries. For safety's sake, replace the batteries every month with the best quality batteries available.

FEEDING TIPS

You will probably start feeding your pup the same food that he has been getting from the breeder; the breeder should give you a few days' supply to start you off. Although you should not give your pup too many treats, you will want to have puppy treats on hand for coaxing, training, rewards, etc. Be careful, though, as a small pup's calorie requirements are relatively low and a few treats can add up to almost a full day's worth of calories without the required nutrition.

are and hopefully to get company out of it. Place your pup in his new bed or crate in his room and close the door. Mercifully, he may fall asleep without a peep. When the inevitable occurs, ignore the whining: he is fine. Be strong and keep his best interest in mind. Do not allow your heart to become guilty and visit the pup. He will fall asleep.

Many breeders recommend placing a piece of bedding from his former home in his new bed so that he recognizes the scent of his littermates. Others still advise placing a hot water bottle in his bed for warmth. This latter may be a good idea provided the pup doesn't attempt to suckle—he'll get good and wet and may not fall asleep so fast.

Puppy's first night can be somewhat stressful for the pup and his new family. Remember that you are setting the tone of nighttime at your house. Unless you want to play with your pup every night at 10 p.m., midnight and 2 a.m., don't initiate the habit. Your family will thank you, and so will your pup!

PREVENTING PUPPY PROBLEMS

SOCIALIZATION

Now that you have done all of the preparatory work and have helped your pup get accustomed to his new home and family, it is about time for you to have some fun! Socializing your Dogo Argentino pup gives you the opportunity to show off your new friend, and your pup gets to reap the benefits of being an adorable creature that people will want to pet and, in general, think is absolutely precious!

Besides getting to know his new family, your puppy should be exposed to other people, animals

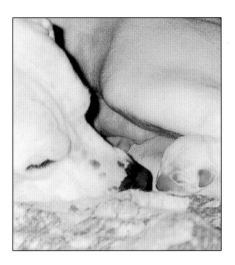

affection, handling and exposure to other animals.

Once your pup has received his necessary vaccinations, feel free to take him out and about (on his lead, of course). Walk him around the neighborhood, take him on your daily errands, let people pet him, let him meet other dogs and pets, etc. Puppies do not have to try to make friends; there will be no shortage of people who will want to introduce themselves. Just make sure

Your Dogo puppy spent the first eight weeks of his life sleeping close to his dam and littermates. The first night in a strange environment can be stressful for any puppy.

and situations, but of course he must not come into close contact with dogs you don't know well until his course of injections is fully complete. This will help him become well adjusted as he grows up and less prone to being timid or fearful of the new things he will encounter. Your pup's socialization began at the breeder's but now it is your responsibility to continue it. The socialization he receives up until the age of 12 weeks is the most critical, as this is the time when he forms his impressions of the outside world. Be especially careful during the eight-to-ten-week period, also known as the fear period. The interaction he receives during this time should be gentle and reassuring. Lack of socialization can manifest itself in fear and aggression as the dog grows up. He needs lots of human contact,

PUPPY PROBLEMS
The majority of problems that are commonly seen in young pups will disappear as your dog gets older. However, how you deal with problems when he is young will determine how he reacts to discipline as an adult dog. It is important to establish who is boss (ideally it will be you!) right away when you are first bonding with your dog. This bond will set the tone for the rest of your life together.

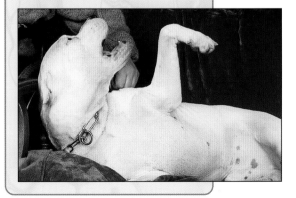

A treat helps to get the puppy's attention for training lessons.

entirely up to you! Your pup's intuitive quest for dominance, coupled with the fact that it is nearly impossible to look at an adorable Dogo Argentino pup with his "puppy-dog" eyes and not cave in, give the pup almost an unfair advantage in getting the upper hand! A pup will definitely test the waters to see what he can

that you carefully supervise each meeting. If the neighborhood children want to say hello, for example, that is great—children and pups most often make great companions. Sometimes an excited child can unintentionally handle a pup too roughly, or an overzealous pup can playfully nip a little too hard. You want to make socialization experiences positive ones. What a pup learns during this very formative stage will affect his attitude toward future encounters. You want your dog to be comfortable around everyone. A pup that has a bad experience with a child may grow up to be a dog that is shy around or aggressive toward children.

CONSISTENCY IN TRAINING

Dogs, being pack animals, naturally need a leader, or else they try to establish dominance in their packs. When you bring a dog into your family, the choice of who becomes the leader and who becomes the "pack" is

PUP MEETS WORLD

Thorough socialization includes not only meeting new people but also being introduced to new experiences such as riding in the car, having his coat brushed, hearing the television, walking in a crowd—the list is endless. The more your pup experiences, and the more positive the experiences are, the less of a shock and the less frightening it will be for your pup to encounter new things.

and cannot do. Do not give in to those pleading eyes—stand your ground when it comes to disciplining the pup and make sure that all family members do the same. It will only confuse the pup when Mother tells him to get off the couch when he is used to sitting up there with Father to watch the nightly news. Avoid discrepancies by having all members of the household decide on the rules before the pup even comes home...and be consistent in enforcing them! Early training shapes the dog's personality, so you cannot be unclear in what you expect.

COMMON PUPPY PROBLEMS

The best way to prevent puppy problems is to be proactive in stopping an undesirable behavior as soon as it starts. The old saying "You can't teach an old dog new tricks" does not necessarily hold true, but it is true that it is much easier to discourage bad behavior in a young developing pup than to wait until the pup's bad behavior

becomes the adult dog's bad habit. There are some problems that are especially prevalent in puppies as they develop.

NIPPING

As puppies start to teethe, they feel the need to sink their teeth into anything available...unfortunately that includes your fingers, arms, hair and toes. You may find this behavior cute for the first five seconds...until you feel just how sharp those puppy teeth are. This is something you want to discourage immediately and consistently with a firm "No!" (or whatever number of firm "Nos" it takes for

The breeder begins the socialization process with very young pups by interacting with them and gently handling them.

him to understand that you mean business). Then replace your finger with an appropriate chew toy. While this behavior is merely annoying when the dog is young, it can become dangerous as your Dogo Argentino's adult teeth grow in and his jaws develop, and he continues to think it is okay to gnaw on human appendages. Your Dogo Argentino does not mean any harm with a friendly nip, but he also does not know his own strength.

CRYING/WHINING

Your pup will often cry, whine, whimper, howl or make some type of commotion when he is left alone. This is basically his way of calling out for attention to make sure that you know he is there and that you have not forgotten about him. He feels insecure when he is left alone, when you are out of the house and he is in his crate or when you are in

Crate training is a necessary ingredient in the making of a well-behaved dog.

TRAINING TIP
Training your puppy takes much patience and can be frustrating at times, but you should see results from your efforts. If you have a puppy that seems untrainable, take him to a trainer or behaviorist. The dog may have a personality problem that requires the help of a professional, or perhaps you need help in learning how to train your dog.

another part of the house and he cannot see you. The noise he is making is an expression of the anxiety he feels at being alone, so he needs to be taught that being alone is okay. You are not actually training the dog to stop making noise, you are training him to feel comfortable when he is alone and thus removing the need for him to make the noise. This is where the crate with cozy bedding and a toy comes in handy. You want to know that he is safe when you are not there to supervise, and you know that he will be safe in his crate rather than roaming freely

CHEWING TIPS

Chewing goes hand in hand with nipping in the sense that a teething puppy is always looking for a way to soothe his aching gums. In this case, instead of chewing on you, he may have taken a liking to your favorite shoe or something else that he should not be chewing. Again, realize that this is a normal canine behavior that does not need to be discouraged, only redirected. Your pup just needs to be taught what is acceptable to chew on and what is off-limits. Consistently tell him "No!" when you catch him chewing on something forbidden and give him a chew toy.

Conversely, praise him when you catch him chewing on something appropriate. In this way, you are discouraging the inappropriate behavior and reinforcing the desired behavior. The puppy's chewing should stop after his adult teeth have come in, but an adult dog continues to chew for various reasons—perhaps because he is bored, needs to relieve tension or just likes to chew. That is why it is important to redirect his chewing when he is still young.

about the house. In order for the pup to stay in his crate without making a fuss, he needs to be comfortable in his crate. On that note, it is extremely important that the crate is never used as a form of punishment, or the pup will have a negative association with the crate.

Accustom the pup to the crate in short, gradually increasing time intervals in which you put him in the crate, maybe with a treat, and stay in the room with him. If he cries or makes a fuss, do not go to him, but stay in his sight. Gradually he will realize that staying in his crate is just fine without your help, and it will not be so traumatic for him when you are not around. You may want to leave the radio on softly when you leave the house; the sound of human voices may be comforting to him.

Pups learn the rules of the pack by interacting with their littermates... who will be "top dog"?

Your Dogo will love to be near you and will spend as much time by your side as you allow him.

DOGO ARGENTINO

DIETARY AND FEEDING CONSIDERATIONS

Today the choices of food for your dog are many and varied. There are simply dozens of brands of food in all sorts of flavors and textures, ranging from puppy diets to those for seniors. There are even hypoallergenic and low-calorie diets available. Because your Dogo's food has a bearing on coat, health and temperament, it is essential that the most suitable diet is selected for a Dogo of his age. It is fair to say, however, that even dedicated owners can be somewhat perplexed by the enormous range of foods available. Only understanding what is best for your dog will help you reach a valued decision.

Every dog owner has his own theory on proper feeding. My personal approach is to try different types of commercial dog food until you find one that seems to be effective and stick with it (i.e., a brand that the dog will eat, will keep him nourished and will not cause excessive flatulence!). I don't believe that a dog needs a variety of foods to stay fit and happy. In reality, the more foods you introduce to the dog, the more finicky he becomes. Ask anyone who feeds their dog table scraps—once you start that habit, you can forget feeding from cans or bags.

Dog foods are produced in three basic types: dry, semi-moist and canned. Dry foods are useful for the cost-conscious for overall they tend to be less expensive than semi-moist or canned. These contain the least fat and the most preservatives. In general, canned

STORING DOG FOOD

You must store your dry dog food carefully. Open packages of dog food quickly lose their vitamin value, usually within 90 days of being opened. Mold spores and vermin could also contaminate the food.

The Dogo dam, blessed with a large and hungry litter, has a plentiful milk supply to feed her nursing puppies.

foods are made up of 60–70% water, while semi-moist ones often contain so much sugar that they are the least preferred by owners, even though their dogs seem to like them.

If you have the time and patience to prepare your dog's meals, then by all means do so. Be sure to include plenty of proteins, carbohydrates and vitamins to keep your canine nourished. I would resist trying to feed the dog dry food on occasion and people food at other times. A dog's digestive system is not like a human's; in fact it is much simpler and relies on consistency for efficiency. Feeding table scraps to the dog who normally eats commercial dry dog food will almost always result in a dog that begs constantly at the supper table.

When selecting your dog's diet, three stages of development must be considered: the puppy stage, the adult stage and the senior stage.

PUPPY STAGE

Puppies instinctively want to suck milk from their dam's teats and a normal puppy will exhibit this behavior from just a few moments following birth. If puppies do not attempt to suckle within the first half-hour or so, the breeder encourages the puppies to do so by placing them on a nipple, having selected ones with plenty of milk. This early milk supply is important in providing colostrum to protect the puppies during the first eight to ten weeks of their lives. Although a dam's milk is much better than any milk formula, despite there being some excellent ones available, if the puppies do not feed the breeder will have to feed them himself. For those with less experience, advice from a veterinarian is important so that you feed not only the right quantity of milk but that of correct quality, fed at suitably frequent intervals, usually every two hours during the first few days of life.

Puppies should be allowed to

TEST FOR PROPER DIET

A good test for proper diet is the color, odor and firmness of your dog's stool. A healthy dog usually produces three semi-hard stools per day. The stools should have no unpleasant odor. They should be the same color from excretion to excretion.

FOOD PREFERENCE

Selecting the best dry dog food is difficult. There is no majority consensus among veterinary scientists as to the value of nutrient analysis (protein, fat, fiber, moisture, ash, cholesterol, minerals, etc.). All agree that feeding trials are what matter most, but you also have to consider the individual dog. The dog's weight, age and activity level, and what pleases his taste, all must be considered. It is probably best to take the advice of your veterinarian. Every dog has individual dietary requirements, and should be fed accordingly.

If your dog is fed a good dry food, he does not require supplements of meat or vegetables. Dogs do appreciate a little variety in their diets, so you may choose to stay with the same brand but vary the flavor. Alternatively, you may wish to add a little flavored stock to give a difference to the taste.

nurse from their dam for about the first six weeks, although from the third or fourth week the breeder begins to introduce small portions of suitable solid food. Most breeders like to introduce alternate milk and meat meals initially, building up to weaning time.

By the time the puppies are seven or a maximum of eight weeks old, they should be fully weaned and fed solely on a

The breeder introduces the litter to solid foods by the third or fourth week.

GRAIN-BASED DIETS

Some less expensive dog foods are based on grains and other plant proteins. While these products may appear to be attractively priced, many breeders prefer a diet based on animal proteins and believe that they are more conducive to your dog's health. Many grain-based diets rely on soy protein, which may cause flatulence (passing gas).

There are many cases, however, when your dog might require a special diet. These special requirements should only be recommended by your veterinarian.

proprietary puppy food. Selection of the most suitable, good-quality diet at this time is essential for a puppy's fastest growth rate is during the first year of life. Dogo Argentino pups should be fed three meals per day when they are six to eight weeks of age. At eight weeks, the pup can be fed twice per day. Be sure not to overfeed your Dogo. Keep the dogs about 20% "thin" to avoid stressing the young dog's joints and ligaments. Fussy eaters may require an additional smaller meal to maintain a good weight.

Veterinarians are usually able to offer advice in this regard and, although the frequency of meals will have been reduced over time, only when a young dog has

reached the age of about 12-18 months should an adult diet be fed. Puppy and junior diets should be well balanced for the needs of your dog, so that except in certain circumstances additional vitamins, minerals and proteins will not be required.

ADULT DIETS

A dog is considered an adult when he has stopped growing, so in general the diet of a Dogo Argentino can be changed to an adult one at about 12-18 months of age, depending on the individual dog. Again you should rely upon your veterinarian or breeder to recommend an acceptable maintenance diet. Major dog-food manufacturers specialize in this type of food and it is just necessary for you to select the one best suited to your dog's needs. Active dogs may have different requirements than sedate dogs.

A Dogo Argentino is fully mature around 12 months of age, though it often takes another 12 to 18 months for the dog to reach his peak as a performance animal.

SENIOR DIETS

As dogs get older, their metabolism changes. The older dog usually exercises less, moves more slowly and sleeps more. This change in lifestyle and physiological performance requires a change in diet. Since these changes take place slowly, they might not be recognizable. What is easily recognizable is weight gain. By continually feeding your dog an adult-maintenance diet when he is slowing down metabolically, your dog will gain weight. Obesity in an older dog compounds the health problems that already accompany old age.

As your dog gets older, few of his organs function up to par. The kidneys slow down and the intestines become less efficient. These age-related factors are best handled with a change in diet and a change in feeding schedule to give smaller portions that are more easily digested.

There is no single best diet for every older dog. While many dogs do well on light or senior diets, other dogs do better on puppy diets or other special premium diets such as lamb and rice. Be sensitive to your senior Dogo Argentino's diet and this will help control other problems that may arise with your old friend.

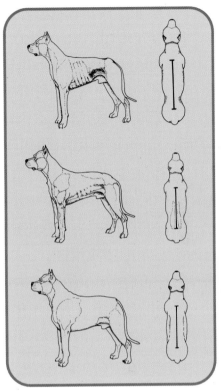

The Dogo Argentino must be kept in optimal condition. From top to bottom, these are top and side views of an underweight, normal weight, and overweight dog.

WATER

Just as your dog needs proper nutrition from his food, water is an essential "nutrient" as well. Water keeps the dog's body properly hydrated and promotes normal function of the body's systems. During housebreaking it is necessary to keep an eye on how much water your Dogo Argentino is drinking, but once he is reliably trained he should have access to clean fresh water at all times. Make sure that the dog's water bowl is clean, and change the water often.

Water is a necessity for every living creature. Provide water indoors and out for your Dogo, being especially aware on warm days.

EXERCISE

All dogs require some form of exercise, regardless of breed. A sedentary lifestyle is as harmful to a dog as it is to a person. The Dogo Argentino happens to be an above-active breed that requires more exercise than most breeds. Regular walks, play sessions in the yard and letting the dog run free in a securely enclosed area under your supervision are all sufficient forms of exercise for the Dogo Argentino. For those who are more ambitious, you will find that your Dogo Argentino will be able to keep up with you on your morning run or evening bike ride. Not only is exercise essential to keep the dog's body fit, it is essential to his mental well-being. A bored Dogo will always find something to do, which often manifests itself in unfathomable destructive behavior. These are big dogs with big paws and jaws—when bored, they can do big damage! In this sense, exercise and entertaining the Dogo are essential for the owner's mental well-being as well!

GROOMING

The Dogo's high threshold of tolerance is a groomer's dream. If you have any experience trying to strip a terrier or clip and bathe a Poodle, then you will truly appreciate the Dogo Argentino. Because of the short hair, coupled with the Dogo's high pain tolerance, it's very necessary to inspect the skin, ears and paws immediately after returning from an outdoor jaunt. The skin is especially sensitive to overexposure and will get sunburned if the dog is not monitored. Sunburn is doubly problematic because Dogos will quietly bask in the warm sun for hours. As much as you'd hate to disturb your companion, try to keep him from lying out for too long. A sunscreen lotion for protection is advised for Dogos that are exposed to the sun regularly.

BRUSHING

The white short-haired coat of the Dogo Argentino gives the breed a magnificent elegance. Practically speaking, this coat is both a joy and a nuisance to the owner. A joy because very little shedding occurs, the hair is hypo-allergenic, and requires little more than a quick daily brushing (lazy owners can actually get away with a weekly brushing without much problem).

A natural bristle brush or a hound glove can be used for regular routine brushing. Daily brushing is effective for removing dead hair and stimulating the dog's natural oils to add shine and a healthy look to the coat. Regular grooming sessions are also a good way to spend time with your dog. Many dogs like the feel of being brushed and will enjoy the daily routine. Be sure to examine the paws for foreign matter and excessive dirt, and keep the nails clipped.

BATHING

The problem with this coat is how quickly it soils, especially when the Dogo Argentino is outside playing for more than ten

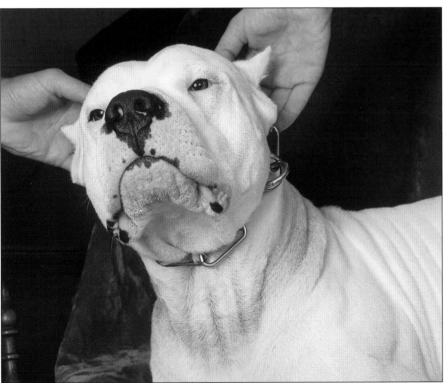

Dogos are easily groomed because they love to be handled by their owners and enjoy any attention their owners will give them.

Dogos need minimal brushing, but they should be brushed regularly to remove dead hairs. Pet shops have a wide selection of brushes and other grooming supplies.

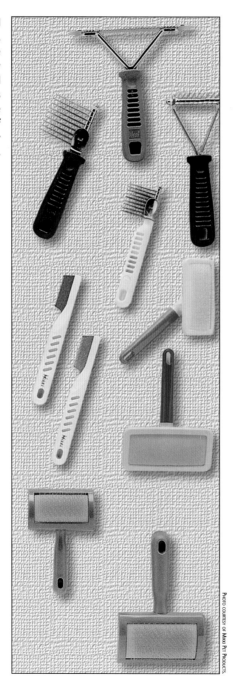

PHOTO COURTESY OF MIKKI PET PRODUCTS.

minutes! The Dogo will dig to Argentina if left to do so, and for some reason, enjoys rolling in the pile of dirt that is accumulated next to the hole. (Strangely enough, Dogos rarely bury anything; they just seem to love digging!) So you can imagine the fun an owner has trying to keep that coarse white coat shiny and clean.

Regular bathing is essential for healthy skin and a healthy, shiny coat. Though not exactly fond of water, the Dogo will have no qualms about a daily bath (or two if necessary!). Unlike many breeds, the Dogo will have no difficulty engaging in an outdoor hosing or a traditional tub bath. Once he experiences the cleaning

GROOMING EQUIPMENT

How much grooming equipment you purchase will depend on how much grooming you are going to do. Here are some basics:
• Pin brush
• Metal comb
• Scissors
• Rubber mat
• Dog shampoo
• Spray hose attachment
• Towels
• Blow dryer
• Ear cleaner
• Cotton balls
• Nail clippers
• Dental-care products

BATHING BEAUTY

Once you are sure that the dog is thoroughly rinsed, squeeze the excess water out of his coat with your hand and dry him with an heavy towel. You may choose to use a blow dryer on his coat or just let it dry naturally. In cold weather, never allow your dog outside with a wet coat.

There are "dry bath" products on the market, which are sprays and powders intended for spot cleaning, that can be used between regular baths if necessary. They are not substitutes for regular baths, but they are easy to use for touch-ups as they do not require rinsing.

ordeal for both of you!

Brush your Dogo Argentino thoroughly to get rid of any dust and dead hair before wetting his coat. Make sure that your dog has a good non-slip surface to stand on. Begin by wetting the dog's coat. A shower or hose attachment is necessary for thoroughly wetting and rinsing the coat.

Next, apply shampoo to the dog's coat and work it into a good lather. You should purchase a shampoo that is made for dogs. Do not use a product made for human

routine a few times, the Dogo will come to a complete understanding that this is something that has to be done and won't give you too much trouble. The only requisite is that you use warm water; the Dogo will not react well to cold or hot water. Frequency of bathing depends mostly on the season, the amount of outdoor activity, and the frequency that the dog rolls in the mud. The bright white fur will give you an obvious indication of when it's time to clean.

Again, like most anything, if you accustom your pup to being bathed as a puppy, it will be second nature by the time he grows up. You want your dog to be at ease in the bathtub or else it could end up a wet, soapy, messy

Keeping a white dog white will require regular baths, especially after your Dogo has been playing in mud or sand.

SOAP IT UP

The use of human soap products like shampoo, bubble bath and hand soap can be damaging to a dog's coat and skin. Human products are too strong; they remove the protective oils coating the dog's hair and skin that make him water-resistant. Use only shampoo made especially for dogs. You may like to use a medicated shampoo, which will help to keep external parasites at bay.

hair. Wash the head last; you do not want shampoo to drip into the dog's eyes while you are washing the rest of his body. Work the shampoo all the way down to the skin. You can use this opportunity to check the skin for any bumps, bites or other abnormalities. Do not neglect any area of the body—get all of the hard-to-reach places.

Once the dog has been thoroughly shampooed, he requires an equally thorough rinsing. Shampoo left in the coat can be irritating to the skin. Protect his eyes from the shampoo by shielding them with your hand and directing the flow of water in the opposite direction. You should also avoid getting water in the ear canal. Be prepared for your dog to shake out his coat—you might want to stand back, but make sure you have a hold on the dog to keep him from running through the house.

Trimming your Dogo's nails is necessary unless the dog wears them down himself. Dogos are fairly tolerant of the nail clipping procedure.

EAR CLEANING

The ears and head are especially susceptible to sunburn and infections. (This is true whether the dog's ears are cropped or not.) The ears should be kept clean and any excess hair inside the ear should be trimmed. Ears can be cleaned with a cotton ball and special cleaner or ear powder made especially for dogs. Constant monitoring of the ears and immediate removal of dirt, mites or other foreign materials will help prevent infections. Find a suitable cream for treatment of sunburn, and watch your dog's ears carefully.

Be on the lookout for any signs of infection or ear-mite

infestation. If your Dogo Argentino has been shaking his head or scratching at his ears frequently, this usually indicates a problem. If his ears have an unusual odor, this is a sure sign of mite infestation or infection, and a signal to have his ears checked by the veterinarian.

NAIL CLIPPING

If you've ever clipped a dog's nails, you will be absolutely amazed at how calm the Dogo is when you're performing this task. Keep the nails trimmed, but not too short, and avoid causing any bleeding.

Your Dogo Argentino should be accustomed to having his nails trimmed at an early age, since it will be a part of your maintenance routine throughout his life. Not only does it look nicer, but a dog with long nails can cause injury if he jumps up or if he scratches someone unintentionally. Also, a long nail has a better chance of ripping and bleeding, or causing the feet to spread. A good rule of thumb is that if you can hear your dog's nails' clicking on the floor when he walks, his nails are too long.

Before you start cutting, make sure you can identify the "quick" in each nail. The quick is a blood vessel that runs through the center of each nail and grows rather close to the end. It will bleed if accidentally cut, which

PEDICURE TIP
A dog that spends a lot of time outside on a hard surface, such as cement or pavement, will have his nails naturally worn down and may not need to have them trimmed as often, except maybe in the colder months when he is not outside as much. Regardless, it is best to get your dog accustomed to the nail-trimming procedure at an early age so that he is used to it. Some dogs are especially sensitive about having their feet touched, but if a dog has experienced it since puppyhood, it should not bother him.

will be quite painful for the dog as it contains nerve endings. Keep some type of clotting agent on hand, such as a styptic pencil or styptic powder (the type used for shaving). This will stop the bleeding quickly when applied to the end of the cut nail. Do not panic if this happens, just stop the bleeding and talk soothingly to your dog. Once he has calmed down, move on to the next nail. It is better to clip a little at a time, particularly with black-nailed dogs.

Hold your pup steady as you begin trimming his nails; you do not want him to make any sudden movements or run away. Talk to him soothingly and stroke him as you clip. Holding his foot in your hand, simply take off the end of each nail in one quick clip. You can purchase nail clippers that are specially made for dogs; you can probably find them wherever you buy grooming supplies.

TRAVELING WITH YOUR DOGO

CAR TRAVEL

You should accustom your Dogo Argentino to riding in a car at an early age. You may or may not take him in the car often, but at

Let sleeping dogs lie! Trim his nails later, though a drowsy Dogo may be more cooperative.

TRAVEL TIP
The most extensive travel you do with your dog may be limited to trips to the vet's office—or you may decide to bring him along for long distances when the family goes on vacation. Whichever the case, it is important to consider your dog's safety while traveling.

the very least he will need to go to the vet and you do not want these trips to be traumatic for the dog or troublesome for you. The safest way for a puppy to ride in the car is in his crate. If he uses a crate in the house, you can use the same crate for travel.

Put the pup in the crate and see how he reacts. If he seems uneasy, you can have a passenger hold him on his lap while you drive. Of course, this will not work when the Dogo is full grown so it is best to accustom him to a crate or a specially made safety harness for dogs, which straps the dog in much like a seat belt. Do not let the dog roam loose in the vehicle—this is very dangerous! If you should stop short, your dog can be thrown and injured. If the dog starts climbing on you and pestering you while you are driving, you will not be able to concentrate on the road. It is an unsafe situation for everyone— human and canine.

For long trips, be prepared to stop to let the dog relieve himself. Take along whatever you need to clean up after him, including some paper towels and perhaps some old bath towels for use should he have a potty accident in the car or suffer from motion sickness.

AIR TRAVEL

Contact your chosen airline before proceeding with your travel plans that include your Dogo. The dog will be required to travel in a fiberglass crate and you should always check in advance with the airline regarding specific requirements for the crate's size, type and labeling. To help put the dog at ease, give him one of his favorite toys in the crate. Do not feed the dog for several hours prior to checking in so that you minimize his need to relieve himself. However, some airlines require that the dog must be fed within four hours of arriving at the airport, in which case a light meal is best.

Make sure your dog is properly identified and that your

IDENTIFICATION OPTIONS

As puppies become more and more expensive, especially those puppies of high quality for showing and/or breeding, they have a greater chance of being stolen. The usual collar dog tag is, of course, easily removed. But there are two more permanent techniques that have become widely used for identification.

The puppy microchip implantation involves the injection of a small microchip, about the size of a corn kernel, under the skin of the dog. If your dog shows up at a clinic or shelter, or is offered for resale under less-than-savory circumstances, it can be positively identified by the microchip. The microchip is scanned, and a registry quickly identifies you as the owner.

Tattooing is done on various parts of the dog, from his belly to his ears. The number tattooed can be your telephone number, your dog's registration number or any other number that you can easily memorize. When professional dog thieves see a tattooed dog, they usually lose interest. For the safety of our dogs, no laboratory facility or dog broker will accept a tattooed dog as stock.

Discuss microchipping and tattooing with your veterinarian and breeder. Some vets perform these services on their own premises for a reasonable fee. To ensure that your dog's identification is effective, be certain that the dog is then properly registered with a legitimate national database.

Select a boarding kennel convenient to your home. The kennel should be neat, clean and spacious, and have a program that will enable your dog to be exercised properly.

TRAVEL TIP
When traveling, never let your dog off-lead in a strange area. Your dog could run away out of fear, decide to chase a passing squirrel or cat or simply want to stretch his legs without restriction—if any of these happen, you might never see your canine friend again.

contact information appears on his ID tags and on his crate. Your Dogo will travel in a different area of the plane than the passengers, so every rule must be strictly followed to prevent the risk of getting separated from your dog.

BOARDING
So you want to take a family vacation—and you want to include *all* members of the family. You would probably make arrangements for accommodations ahead of time anyway, but this is especially important when traveling with a dog. You do not want to make an overnight stop at the only place around for miles and find out that they do not allow dogs. Also, you do not want to reserve a place for

your family without confirming that you are traveling with a dog because if it is against their policy you may not have a place to stay.

Alternatively, if you are traveling and choose not to take your Dogo Argentino, you will have to make arrangements for him while you are away. Some options are to take him to a friend's house to stay while you are gone, to have a familiar trusted friend stop by often or stay at your house, or, although the author does not recommend it unless absolutely necessary, take your dog to a reputable boarding kennel. If you choose to board him at a kennel, you should visit in advance to see the facilities, how clean they are and where the dogs are kept. Talk to some of the employees and see how they treat the dogs—do they spend time with the dogs, play with them, exercise them, etc.? Also find out the kennel's policy on vaccinations and what they require. This is for all of the dogs' safety, since when dogs are kept together, there is a greater risk of diseases being passed from dog to dog.

COLLAR REQUIRED

If your dog gets lost, he is not able to ask for directions home. Identification tags fastened to the collar give important information—the dog's name, the owner's name, the owner's address and a telephone number where the owner can be reached. This makes it easy for whomever finds the dog to contact the owner and arrange to have the dog returned. An added advantage is that a person will be more likely to approach a lost dog who has ID tags on his collar; it tells the person that this is somebody's pet rather than a stray. This is the easiest and fastest method of identification, provided that the tags stay on the collar and the collar stays on the dog.

IDENTIFICATION

Your Dogo Argentino is your valued companion and friend. That is why you always keep a close eye on him and you have made sure that he cannot escape from the yard or wriggle out of his collar and run away from you. However, accidents can happen and there may come a time when your dog unexpectedly gets separated from you. If this unfortunate event should occur, the first thing on your mind will be finding him. Proper identification, including an ID tag, a tattoo, and possibly a microchip, will increase the chances of his being returned to you safely and quickly.

Your Dogo should never be without a collar, to which is attached a suitable identification tag.

TRAINING YOUR
DOGO ARGENTINO

As the breed standard states, the Dogo Argentino is "incredibly obedient and willing to please," yet "he is extremely sensitive to his handler and cannot tolerate forceful training methods." Without a doubt, the Dogo is an intelligent canine—the breed standard actually cites "lack of intelligence" as a breed fault, a phrase rarely used in breed standards. The owner and handler of a Dogo Argentino must be aware of the breed's high level of intelligence and desire to please, and therefore act kindly and considerately to the Dogo and train the dog with patience and sensitivity.

Before you start actually teaching commands, teach your Dogo good manners as you learn how and why he behaves the way he does. Find out how to communicate with your dog and how to recognize and understand his communications with you. In no time, he will become smart, interesting, well behaved and fun to be with. He demonstrates his bond of devotion to you daily. In other words, your Dogo Argentino does wonders for your ego because he constantly reminds you that you are not only his leader, you are his hero!

Those involved with teaching dog obedience and counseling owners about their dogs' behavior have discovered some

REAP THE REWARDS
If you start with a normal, healthy dog and give him time, patience and some carefully executed lessons, you will reap the rewards of that training for the life of the dog. And what a life it will be! The two of you will find immeasurable pleasure in the companionship you have built together with love, respect and understanding.

interesting facts about dog ownership. For example, training dogs when they are puppies results in the highest rate of success in developing well-mannered and well-adjusted adult dogs. Training an older dog, from six months to six years of age, can produce almost equal results providing that the owner accepts the dog's slower rate of learning capability and is willing to work patiently to help the dog succeed at developing to his fullest potential. Unfortunately, many owners of untrained adult dogs lack the patience factor, so they do not persist until their dogs are successful at learning particular behaviors.

Training a puppy aged 10 to 16 weeks (20 weeks at the most) is like working with a dry sponge in a pool of water. The pup soaks up whatever you show him and constantly looks for more things to do and learn. At this early age, his body is not yet producing hormones, and therein lies the reason for such a high rate of success. Without hormones, he is focused on his owners and not particularly interested in investigating other places, dogs, people, etc. You are his leader: his provider of food, water, shelter and security. He latches onto you and wants to stay close. He will usually follow you from room to room, will not let you out of his sight

THE HAND THAT FEEDS

To a dog's way of thinking, your hands are like his mouth in terms of a defense mechanism. If you squeeze him too tightly, he might just bite you because that would be his normal response. This is not aggressive biting and, although all biting should be discouraged, you need the discipline in learning how to handle your dog.

when you are outdoors with him and will respond in like manner to the people and animals you encounter. If you greet a friend warmly, he will be happy to

PARENTAL GUIDANCE

Training a dog is a life experience. Many parents admit that much of what they know about raising children they learned from caring for their dogs. Dogs respond to love, fairness and guidance, just as children do. Become a good dog owner and you may become an even better parent.

greet the person as well. If, however, you are hesitant, even anxious, about the approach of a stranger, he will respond accordingly.

Once the puppy begins to produce hormones, his natural curiosity emerges and he begins to investigate the world around him. It is at this time when you may notice that the untrained dog begins to wander away from you and even ignore your commands to stay close.

There are usually classes within a reasonable distance of the owner's home, but you can also do a lot to train your dog yourself. Sometimes there are classes available but the tuition is too costly. Whatever the circumstances, the solution to the problem of training your Dogo without the advantage of formal obedience classes lies within the pages of this book.

This chapter is devoted to helping you train your Dogo Argentino at home. If the recommended procedures are followed faithfully, you may expect positive results that will prove rewarding to both you and your dog.

Whether your new charge is a puppy or a mature adult, the methods of teaching and the techniques we use in training basic behaviors are the same. After all, no dog, whether puppy or adult, likes harsh or inhu-

Part of being a well-behaved canine citizen is getting along with other dogs. This is especially important with a breed like the Dogo Argentino that tends to be dog-aggressive.

THINK BEFORE YOU BARK
Dogs are sensitive to their masters' moods and emotions. Use your voice wisely when communicating with your dog. Never raise your voice at your dog unless you are trying to correct him. "Barking" at your dog can become as meaningless as "dogspeak" is to you.

mane methods. All creatures, however, respond favorably to gentle motivational methods and sincere praise.

HOUSEBREAKING
You can train a puppy to relieve himself wherever you choose, but this must be somewhere suitable. You should bear in mind from the outset that when your puppy is old enough to go out in public places, any canine deposits must be removed at once. You will always have to

carry with you a small plastic bag or "poop-scoop." Outdoor training includes such surfaces as grass, dirt and cement. Indoor training usually means training your dog to newspaper.

When deciding on the surface and location that you will want your Dogo Argentino to use, be sure it is going to be permanent. Training your dog to grass and then changing your mind two months later is extremely difficult for both dog and owner.

Next, choose the command you will use each and every time you want your puppy to void. "Go hurry up" and "Outside!" are examples of commands commonly used by dog owners.

Get in the habit of asking the puppy your chosen relief command before you take him out. That way, when he becomes an adult, you will be able to determine if he wants to go out when you ask him. A confirmation will be signs of interest, such as wagging his tail, watching you intently, going to the door, etc.

Your Dogo should be trained to utilize an acceptable site for relief. The site should be maintained in a clean condition and be as isolated from walking traffic as possible.

PUPPY'S NEEDS

The puppy needs to relieve himself after play periods, after each meal, after he has been sleeping and any time he indicates that he is looking for a place to urinate or defecate. The urinary and intestinal tract muscles of very young puppies are not fully developed. Therefore, like human babies, puppies need to relieve themselves frequently.

Take your puppy out often—every hour for an eight week old, for example. The older the puppy, the less often he will need to relieve himself. Finally,

as a mature healthy adult, he will require only three to five relief trips per day.

HOUSING

Since the types of housing and control you provide for your puppy have a direct relationship on the success of house-training, we consider the various aspects of both before we begin training.

Taking a new puppy home and turning him loose in your house can be compared to turning a child loose in a sports arena and telling the child that the place is all his! The sheer enormity of the place would be too much for him to handle.

Instead, offer the puppy clearly defined areas where he can play, sleep, eat and live. A room of the house where the family gathers is the most obvious choice. Puppies are social

HONOR AND OBEY

Dogs are the most honorable animals in existence. They consider another species (humans) as their own. They interface with you. You are their leader. Puppies perceive children to be on their level; their actions around small children are different from their behavior around their adult masters.

CANINE DEVELOPMENT SCHEDULE

It is important to understand how and at what age a puppy develops into adulthood. If you are a puppy owner, consult the following Canine Development Schedule to determine the stage of development your puppy is currently experiencing. This knowledge will help you as you work with the puppy in the weeks and months ahead.

Period	Age	Characteristics
FIRST TO THIRD	BIRTH TO SEVEN WEEKS	Puppy needs food, sleep and warmth, and responds to simple and gentle touching. Needs mother for security and disciplining. Needs littermates for learning and interacting with other dogs. Pup learns to function within a pack and learns pack order of dominance. Begin socializing pup with adults and children for short periods. Pup begins to become aware of his environment.
FOURTH	EIGHT TO TWELVE WEEKS	Brain is fully developed. Needs socializing with outside world. Remove from mother and littermates. Needs to change from canine pack to human pack. Human dominance necessary. Fear period occurs between 8 and 12 weeks. Avoid fright and pain.
FIFTH	THIRTEEN TO SIXTEEN WEEKS	Training and formal obedience should begin. Less association with other dogs, more with people, places, situations. Period will pass easily if you remember this is pup's change-to-adolescence time. Be firm and fair. Flight instinct prominent. Permissiveness and over-disciplining can do permanent damage. Praise for good behavior.
JUVENILE	FOUR TO EIGHT MONTHS	Another fear period about 7 to 8 months of age. It passes quickly, but be cautious of fright and pain. Sexual maturity reached. Dominant traits established. Dog should understand sit, down, come and stay by now.

NOTE: THESE ARE APPROXIMATE TIME FRAMES. ALLOW FOR INDIVIDUAL DIFFERENCES IN PUPPIES.

PAPER CAPER

Never line your pup's sleeping area with newspaper. Puppy litters are usually raised on newspaper and, once in your home, the puppy will immediately associate newspaper with voiding. Never put newspaper on any floor while house-training, as this will only confuse the puppy. If you are paper-training him, use paper in his designated relief area only. Finally, restrict water intake after evening meals. Offer a few licks at a time—never let a young puppy gulp water after meals.

animals and need to feel a part of the pack right from the start. Hearing your voice, watching you while you are doing things and smelling you nearby are all positive reinforcers that he is now a member of your pack. Usually a family room, the kitchen or a nearby adjoining breakfast area is ideal for providing safety and security for both puppy and owner.

Within that room there should be a smaller area that the puppy can call his own. An alcove, a wire or fiberglass dog crate or a gated corner from which he can view the activities of his new family will be fine. The size of the area or crate is the key factor here. The area must be large enough for the puppy to lie down and stretch out as well as stand up without rubbing his head on the top, yet small enough so that he cannot relieve himself at one end and sleep at the other without coming into contact with his droppings until fully trained to relieve himself outside. The designated area should be lined with clean bedding and a chew toy. Water must always be available, in a non-spill container.

Dogs are, by nature, clean animals and will not remain close to their relief areas unless forced to do so. In those cases, they then become dirty dogs and usually remain that way for life.

CONTROL

By *control*, we mean helping the puppy to create a lifestyle pattern that will be compatible to that of his human pack (*you*!). Just as we guide little children to learn our way of life, we must show the puppy when it is time to play, eat, sleep, exercise and even entertain himself.

Your puppy should always sleep in his crate. He should also learn that, during times of household confusion and excessive human activity such as at breakfast when family members are preparing for the day, he can play by himself in relative safety

ATTENTION!

Your dog is actually training you at the same time you are training him. Dogs do things to get attention. They usually repeat whatever succeeds in getting your attention.

Above all, Dogos like to be comfortable!

This Dogo puppy selected the laundry basket because it carried the scent of his owners and was soft and comfortable.

and comfort in a designated area. Each time you leave the puppy alone, he should understand exactly where he is to stay. Puppies are chewers. They cannot tell the difference between lamp cords, television wires, shoes, table legs and the like. Chewing into a television wire, for example, can be fatal to the puppy while a shorted wire can start a fire in the house.

If the puppy chews on the arm of the chair when he is alone, you will probably discipline him angrily when you get home. Thus, he makes the association that your coming home means he is going to be punished. (He will not remember chewing the chair and is incapable of making the association of the discipline with his naughty deed.)

Other times of excitement, such as visits from friends, family parties, etc., can be fun for the puppy providing he can view the activities from the

security of his crate. He is not underfoot and he is not being fed all sorts of tidbits that will probably cause him stomach distress, yet he still feels a part of the fun.

SCHEDULE
A puppy should be taken to his relief area each time he is released from his designated area, after meals, after a play session and when he first awakens in the morning (at age eight

THE GOLDEN RULE
The golden rule of dog training is simple. For each "question" (command), there is only one correct answer (reaction). One command = one reaction. Keep practicing the command until the dog reacts correctly without hesitating. Be repetitive but not monotonous. Dogs get bored just as people do!

weeks, this can mean 5 a.m.!). The puppy will indicate that he's ready "to go" by circling or sniffing busily—do not misinterpret these signs. For a puppy less than ten weeks of age, a routine of taking him out every hour is necessary. As the puppy grows, he will be able to wait for longer periods of time.

Keep trips to his relief area short. Stay no more than five or six minutes and then return to the house. If he goes during that

An open crate is fine for inside your home. For puppies, however, never put the water bowl inside the crate. This invites accidents when the puppy is crated.

time, praise him lavishly and take him indoors immediately. If he does not, but he has an accident when you go back indoors, pick him up immediately, say "No! No!" and return to his relief area. Wait a few minutes, then return to the house again. Never hit a puppy or put his face in urine or excrement when he has an accident!

Once indoors, put the puppy in his crate until you have had time to clean up his accident. Then release him to the family area and watch him more closely than before. Chances are, his accident was a result of your not picking up his signal or waiting too long before offering him the opportunity to relieve himself. Never hold a grudge against the puppy for accidents.

Let the puppy learn that going outdoors means it is time to relieve himself, not play. Once trained, he will be able to play indoors and out and still differentiate between the times for play versus the times for relief.

Help him develop regular

TAKE THE LEAD

Do not carry your dog to his relief area. Lead him there on a leash or, better yet, encourage him to follow you to the spot. If you start carrying him to his spot, you might end up doing this routine forever and your dog will have the satisfaction of having trained *you*.

HOW MANY TIMES A DAY?

AGE	RELIEF TRIPS
To 14 weeks	10
14–22 weeks	8
22–32 weeks	6
Adulthood	4
(dog stops growing)	

These are estimates, of course, but they are a guide to the *minimum* number of opportunities a dog should have each day to relieve himself.

provide him with undivided attention.

Each time you put a puppy in his own area use the same command, whatever suits best. Soon, he will run to his crate or his own special area when he hears you say those words.

Crate training provides safety for you, the puppy and the home. It also provides the puppy with a feeling of security, and that helps the puppy achieve self-confidence and clean habits.

Remember that one of the primary ingredients in house-training your puppy is control. Regardless of your lifestyle, there will always be occasions when you will need to have a place where your dog can stay and be happy and safe. Crate training is the answer for now and in the future.

In conclusion, a few key elements are really all you need for a successful house-training method—consistency, frequency, praise, control and supervision. By following these procedures with a normal, healthy puppy, you and the puppy will soon be past the stage of "accidents" and ready to move on to a clean and rewarding life together.

ROLES OF DISCIPLINE, REWARD AND PUNISHMENT

Discipline, training one to act in accordance with rules, brings order to life. It is as simple as

hours for naps, being alone, playing by himself and just resting, all in his crate. Encourage him to entertain himself while you are busy with your activities. Let him learn that having you near is comforting, but it is not your main purpose in life to

that. Without discipline, particularly in a group society, chaos reigns supreme and the group will eventually perish. Humans and canines are social animals and need some form of discipline in order to function effectively. They must procure food, protect their home base and their young and reproduce to keep the species going.

If there were no discipline in the lives of social animals, they would eventually die from starvation and/or predation by other stronger animals. In the case of

THE SUCCESS METHOD

Success that comes by luck is usually short-lived. Success that comes by well-thought-out proven methods is often more easily achieved and permanent. This is the Success Method. It is designed to give you, the puppy owner, a simple yet proven way to help your puppy develop clean living habits and a feeling of security in his new environment.

6 Steps to Successful Crate Training

1 Tell the puppy "Crate time!" and place him in the crate with a small treat (a piece of cheese or half of a biscuit). Let him stay in the crate for five minutes while you are in the same room. Then release him and praise lavishly. Never release him when he is fussing. Wait until he is quiet before you let him out.

2 Repeat Step 1 several times a day.

3 The next day, place the puppy in the crate as before. Let him stay there for ten minutes. Do this several times.

4 Continue building time in five-minute increments until the puppy stays in his crate for 30 minutes with you in the room. Always take him to his relief area after prolonged periods in his crate.

5 Now go back to Step 1 and let the puppy stay in his crate for five minutes, this time while you are out of the room.

6 Once again, build crate time in five-minute increments with you out of the room. When the puppy will stay willingly in his crate (he may even fall asleep!) for 30 minutes with you out of the room, he will be ready to stay in it for several hours at a time.

THE CLEAN LIFE

By providing sleeping and resting quarters that fit the dog, and offering frequent opportunities to relieve himself outside his quarters, the puppy quickly learns that the outdoors (or the newspaper if you are training him to paper) is the place to go when he needs to urinate or defecate. It also reinforces his innate desire to keep his sleeping quarters clean. This, in turn, helps develop the muscle control that will eventually produce a dog with clean living habits.

domestic canines, dogs need discipline in their lives in order to understand how their pack (you and other family members) functions and how they must act in order to survive.

A large humane society in a highly populated area recently surveyed dog owners regarding their satisfaction with their relationships with their dogs. People who had trained their dogs were 75% more satisfied with their pets than those who had never trained their dogs.

Dr. Edward Thorndike, a noted psychologist, established *Thorndike's Theory of Learning*, which states that a behavior that results in a pleasant event tends to be repeated. A behavior that results in an unpleasant event tends not to be repeated. It is this theory on which training methods are based today. For example, if you manipulate a dog to perform a specific behavior and reward him for doing it, he is likely to do it again because he enjoyed the end result.

Occasionally, punishment, a penalty inflicted for an offense, is necessary. The best type of punishment often comes from an outside source. For example, a child is told not to touch the stove because he may get burned. He disobeys and touches the stove. In doing so, he receives a burn. From that time on, he respects the heat of the stove and avoids contact with it. Therefore, a behavior that results in an unpleasant event tends not to be repeated.

A good example of a dog learning the hard way is the dog who chases the house cat. He is

This promising puppy has a future filled with successes to look forward to, provided that his owners are patient and persistent.

told many times to leave the cat alone, yet he persists in teasing the cat. Then, one day he begins chasing the cat but the cat turns and swipes a claw across the dog's face, leaving him with a painful gash on his nose. The final result is that the dog stops chasing the cat.

TRAINING EQUIPMENT

COLLAR AND LEAD

For a Dogo Argentino the collar and lead that you use for training must be one with which you are easily able to work, not too heavy for the dog, yet sturdy enough to use with a large, strong breed, and perfectly safe.

TREATS

Have a bag of treats on hand. Something nutritious and easy to swallow works best. Use a soft treat, a chunk of cheese or a piece of cooked chicken rather than a dry biscuit. By the time the dog has finished chewing a dry treat, he will forget why he is being rewarded in the first place! Using food rewards, by the way, will not teach a dog to beg at the table—the only way to teach a dog to beg at the table is to give him food from the table. In training, rewarding the dog with a food treat will help him associate praise and the treats with learning new behaviors that obviously please his owner.

PLAN TO PLAY

The puppy should also have regular play and exercise sessions when he is with you or a family member. Exercise for a very young puppy can consist of a short walk around the house or yard. Playing can include fetching games with a large ball or a special toy. (All puppies teethe and need soft things upon which to chew.) Remember to restrict play periods to indoors within his living area (the family room, for example) until he is completely house-trained.

Once your Dogo has grown up, a sturdy collar and thick leather lead are recommended for daily use.

TRAINING BEGINS: ASK THE DOG A QUESTION

In order to teach your dog anything, you must first get his attention. After all, he cannot learn anything if he is looking away from you with his mind on something else.

To get his attention, ask him, "School?" and immediately walk over to him and give him a treat as you tell him "Good dog." Wait a minute or two and repeat the routine, this time with a treat in your hand as you approach within a foot of the dog. Do not go directly to him, but stop about a foot short of him and hold out the treat as you ask, "School?" He will see you approaching with a treat in your hand and most likely begin walking toward you. As you meet, give him the treat and praise again.

The third time, ask the question, have a treat in your hand and walk only a short distance toward the dog so that he must walk almost all the way to you. As he reaches you, give him the treat and praise again.

By this time, the dog will probably be getting the idea that if he pays attention to you, especially when you ask that question, it will pay off in treats and enjoyable activities for him. In other words, he learns that "school" means doing great things with you that result in treats and positive attention for him.

Remember that the dog does not understand your verbal language, he only recognizes sounds. Your question translates to a series of sounds for him, and those sounds become the signal to go to you and pay attention; if he does, he will get to interact with you plus receive treats and praise.

KEEP SMILING

Never train your dog, puppy or adult, when you are angry or in a sour mood. Dogs are very sensitive to human feelings, especially anger, and if your dog senses that you are angry or upset, he will connect your anger with his training and learn to resent or fear his training sessions.

THE BASIC COMMANDS

TEACHING SIT

Now that you have the dog's attention, attach his lead and hold it in your left hand and a food treat in your right. Place your food hand at the dog's nose and let him lick the treat but not take it from you. Say "Sit" and slowly raise your food hand from in front of the dog's nose up over his head so that he is looking at the ceiling. As he bends his head upward, he will have to bend his knees to maintain his balance. As he bends his knees, he will assume a sit position. At that point, release the food treat and praise lavishly with comments such as "Good dog! Good sit!" Remember to always praise enthusiastically, because dogs relish verbal praise from their owners and feel so proud of themselves whenever they accomplish a behavior.

You will not use food forever in getting the dog to obey your commands. Food is only used to teach new behaviors, and once the dog knows what you want when you give a specific command, you will wean him off the food treats but still maintain the verbal praise. After all, you will always have your voice with you, and there will be many times when you have no food rewards but expect the dog to obey.

TEACHING DOWN

Teaching the down exercise is easy when you understand how the dog perceives the down position, and it is very difficult when you do not. Dogs perceive the down position as a submissive one, therefore teaching the down exercise using a forceful method can sometimes make the dog develop such a fear of the down that he either runs away when you say "Down" or he attempts to snap at the person who tries to force him down.

Have the dog sit alongside your left leg, facing in the same direction as you are. Hold the lead in your left hand and a food treat in your right. Now place your left hand lightly on the top of the dog's shoulders where they meet above the spinal cord. Do not push down on the dog's shoulders; simply

Most trainers recommend the use of food treats to convince the Dogo when teaching new commands.

rest your left hand there so you can guide the dog to lie down close to your left leg rather than to swing away from your side when he drops.

Now place the food hand at the dog's nose, say "Down" very softly (almost a whisper), and slowly lower the food hand to the dog's front feet. When the food hand reaches the floor, begin moving it forward along

> **COMMAND STANCE**
> Stand up straight and authoritatively when giving your dog commands. Do not issue commands when lying on the floor or lying on your back on the sofa. If you are on your hands and knees when you give a command, your dog will think you are positioning yourself to play.

The stay command can be practiced in the sit or down position.

the floor in front of the dog. Keep talking softly to the dog, saying things like, "Do you want this treat? You can do this, good dog." Your reassuring tone of voice will help calm the dog as he tries to follow the food hand in order to get the treat.

When the dog's elbows touch the floor, release the food and praise softly. Try to get the dog to maintain that down position for several seconds before you let him sit up again. The goal here is to get the dog to settle down and not feel threatened in the down position.

TEACHING STAY

It is easy to teach the dog to stay in either a sit or a down position. Again, we use food and praise during the teaching process as we help the dog to understand exactly what it is that we are expecting him to do.

To teach the sit/stay, start with the dog sitting on your left side as before and hold the lead in your left hand. Have a food treat in your right hand and place your food hand at the dog's nose. Say "Stay" and step out on your right foot to stand directly in front of the dog, toe to toe, as he licks and nibbles the treat. Be sure to keep his head facing upward to maintain the sit position. Count to five and then swing around to stand next to the dog again with him on your left. As soon as you get back to the original position, release the food and praise lavishly.

To teach the down/stay, do the down as previously described. As soon as the dog lies down, say "Stay" and step out on your right foot just as you did in the sit/stay. Count to five and then return to stand beside the dog with him on your left side. Release the treat and praise as always.

Within a week or ten days, you can begin to add a bit of distance between you and your dog when you leave him. When you do, use your left hand open with the palm facing the dog as a stay signal, much the same as the hand signal a police officer uses to stop traffic at an intersection. Hold the food treat in your right hand as before, but this time the food is not touching the dog's nose. He will watch the food hand and quickly learn that he is going to get that treat as

DOUBLE JEOPARDY

A dog in jeopardy never lies down. He stays alert on his feet because instinct tells him that he may have to run away or fight for his survival. Therefore, if a dog feels threatened or anxious, he will not lie down. Consequently, it is important to keep the dog calm and relaxed as he learns the down exercise.

If your Dogo is comfortable in the down position, you will have fewer problems teaching this command. The Dogo must never feel threatened or jeopardized.

soon as you return to his side.

When you can stand 1 yard away from your dog for 30 seconds, you can then begin building time and distance in both stays. Eventually, the dog can be expected to remain in the stay position for prolonged periods of time until you return to him or call him to you. Always praise lavishly when he stays.

TEACHING COME

If you make teaching "come" an exciting experience, you should never have a "student" that does not love the game or that fails to come when called. The secret, it seems, is never to teach the word "come."

At times when an owner most wants his dog to come when called, the owner is likely upset or anxious and he allows these feelings to come through in the tone of his voice when he

OBEDIENCE SCHOOL

Taking your dog to an obedience school may be the best investment in time and money you can ever make. You will enjoy the benefits for the lifetime of your dog and you will have the opportunity to meet people who have similar expectations for companion dogs.

calls his dog. Hearing that desperation in his owner's voice, the dog fears the results of going to him and therefore either disobeys outright or runs in the opposite direction. The secret, therefore, is to teach the dog a game and, when you want him to come to you, simply play the game. It is practically a no-fail solution!

To begin, have several members of your family take a few food treats and each go into a different room in the house. Take turns calling the dog, and each person should celebrate the dog's finding him with a treat and lots of happy praise. When a person calls the dog, he is actually inviting the dog to find him

FAMILY TIES
If you have other pets in the home and/or interact often with the pets of friends and other family members, your pup will respond to those pets in much the same manner as you do. It is only when you show fear of or resentment toward another animal that he will act fearful or unfriendly.

Hand signals can be used in conjunction with verbal commands. Once trained, the Dogo will obey either or both.

The dog should begin and end the heel command by sitting at the owner's left side.

and get a treat as a reward for "winning."

A few turns of the "Where are you?" game and the dog will figure out that everyone is playing the game and that each person has a big celebration awaiting his success at locating them. Once he learns to love the game, simply calling out "Where are you?" will bring him running from wherever he is when he hears that all-important question.

The come command is recognized as one of the most important things to teach a dog, but there are trainers who work with thousands of dogs and never teach the actual word "come." Yet these dogs will race to respond to a person who uses the dog's name followed by "Where are you?" For example, a woman has a 12-year-old companion dog who went blind, but who never fails to locate her owner when asked, "Where are you?"

Children particularly love to play this game with their dogs. Children can hide in smaller places like a shower stall or bathtub, behind a bed or under a table. The dog needs to work a little bit harder to find these hiding places, but when he does he loves to celebrate with a treat and a tussle with a favorite youngster.

TEACHING HEEL

Heeling means that the dog walks beside the owner without pulling. It takes time and patience on the owner's part to succeed at teaching the dog that he (the owner) will not proceed unless the dog is walking calmly beside him. Pulling out ahead on the lead is not acceptable.

Begin with holding the lead in your left hand as the dog sits beside your left leg. Move the loop end of the lead to your right hand but keep your left

FETCH!
Play fetching games with your puppy in an enclosed area where he can retrieve his toy and bring it back to you. Always use a toy or object designated just for this purpose. Never use a shoe, sock or other item he may later confuse with those in your closet or underneath your chair.

"WHERE ARE YOU?"

When calling the dog, do not say "Come." Say things like, "Rover, where are you? See if you can find me! I have a biscuit for you!" Keep up a constant line of chatter with coaxing sounds and frequent questions such as, "Where are you?" The dog will learn to follow the sound of your voice to locate you and receive his reward.

hand short on the lead so it keeps the dog in close next to you.

Say "Heel" and step forward on your left foot. Keep the dog close to you and take three steps. Stop and have the dog sit next to you in what we now call the heel position. Praise verbally, but do not touch the dog. Hesitate a moment and

To participate successfully in activities like obedience or agility, shown here, the dog must reliably obey commands off-lead.

begin again with "Heel," taking three steps and stopping, at which point the dog is told to sit again.

Your goal here is to have the dog walk those three steps without pulling on the lead. When he will walk calmly beside you for three steps without pulling, increase the number of steps you take to five. Once he will walk politely beside you while you take five steps, you can increase the length of your walk to ten steps. Keep increasing the length of your stroll until the dog will walk quietly beside you without pulling as long as you want him to heel. When you stop heeling, indicate to the dog that the exercise is over by verbally praising as you pet him and say "OK, good dog." The "OK" is used as a release word, meaning that the exercise is finished and the dog is free to relax.

If you are dealing with a dog who insists on pulling you around, simply "put on your brakes" and stand your ground until the dog realizes that the two of you are not going anywhere until he is beside you and moving at your pace, not his. It may take some time just standing there to convince the dog that you are the leader and you will be the one to decide on the direction and speed of your travel.

Each time the dog looks up

TRY, TRY AGAIN
Dogs are as different from each other as people are. What works for one dog may not work for another. Have an open mind. If one method of training is unsuccessful, try another.

at you or slows down to give a slack lead between the two of you, quietly praise him and say, "Good heel. Good dog." Eventually, the dog will begin to respond and within a few days he will be walking politely beside you without pulling on the lead. At first, the training sessions should be kept short and very positive; soon the dog will be able to walk nicely with you for increasingly longer distances. Remember also to give the dog free time and the opportunity to run and play when you are finished with heel practice.

WEANING OFF FOOD IN TRAINING
Food is used in training new behaviors. Once the dog understands what behavior goes with a specific command, it is time to start weaning him off the food treats. At first, give a treat after each exercise. Then, start to give a treat only after every other exercise. Mix up the times when you offer a food reward and the times when you only offer praise

Dogos are very agile and, if properly trained, can excel in agility trials, where speed and accuracy over a series of obstacles are tested.

so that the dog will never know when he is going to receive both food and praise and when he is going to receive only praise. This is called a variable-ratio reward system and it proves successful because there is always the chance that the owner will produce a treat, so the dog never stops trying for that reward. No matter what, *always* give verbal praise.

OBEDIENCE CLASSES

It is a good idea to enroll in an obedience class if one is available in your area. Many areas have dog clubs that offer basic obedience training as well as preparatory classes for obedience competition. There are also local dog trainers who offer similar classes.

At obedience trials, dogs can earn titles at various levels of competition. The beginning levels of competition include basic behaviors such as sit, down, heel and so on. The more advanced levels of competition include jumping, retrieving, scent discrimination and signal work. The advanced levels

CALM DOWN

Dogs will do anything for your attention. If you reward the dog when he is calm and attentive, you will develop a well-mannered dog. If, on the other hand, you greet your dog excitedly and encourage him to wrestle with you, the dog will greet you the same way and you will have a hyperactive dog on your hands.

require a dog and owner to put a lot of time and effort into their training, and the titles that can be earned at these levels of competition are very prestigious.

OTHER ACTIVITIES FOR LIFE
Whether a dog is trained in the structured environment of a class or alone with his owner at home, there are many activities that can bring fun and rewards to both owner and dog once they have mastered basic control. Teaching the dog to help out around the home, in the yard or on the farm provides great satisfaction to both dog and owner. In addition, the dog's help makes life a little easier for his owner and raises his stature as a valued companion to his family. It helps give the dog a purpose by occupying his mind and providing an outlet for his energy.

Backpacking is an exciting

> **HELPING PAWS**
> Your dog may not be the next Lassie, but every pet has the potential to do some tricks well. Identify his natural talents and hone them. Is your dog always happy and upbeat? Teach him to wag his tail or give you his paw on command. Real home-bodies can be trained to do household chores, such as carrying dirty laundry or retrieving the morning paper.

and healthy activity that the dog can be taught without assistance from more than his owner. The exercise of walking and climbing is good for man and dog alike, and the bond that they develop together is priceless.

If you are interested in participating in organized competition with your Dogo Argentino, there are activities other than obedience in which you and your dog can become involved. Agility is a sport where dogs run through an obstacle course that includes various jumps, tunnels and other exercises to test the dog's speed and coordination. The owners run through the course beside their dogs to give commands and to guide them through the course. Although competitive, the focus is on fun—it's fun to do, fun to watch, and great exercise.

This Dogo skillfully navigates the weave poles at an agility trial.

The Dogo Argentino is truly a "superdog." A well-trained Dogo is capable of excelling in a multitude of activities and, most importantly, of being a devoted and loving pet.

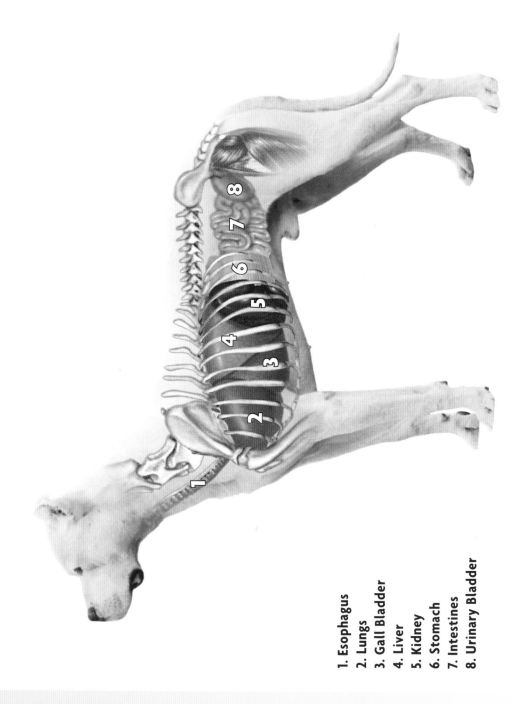

1. Esophagus
2. Lungs
3. Gall Bladder
4. Liver
5. Kidney
6. Stomach
7. Intestines
8. Urinary Bladder

Internal Organs of the Dogo Argentino

Dogs suffer from many of the same physical illnesses as people. They might even share many of the same psychological problems. Since people usually know more about human diseases than canine maladies, many of the terms used in this chapter will be familiar but not necessarily those used by veterinarians. We will use the term *x-ray*, instead of the more acceptable term *radiograph*. We will also use the familiar term *symptoms* even though dogs don't have symptoms, which are verbal descriptions of the patient's feelings: dogs have *clinical signs*. Since dogs can't speak, we have to look for clinical signs...but we still use the term *symptoms* in this book.

As a general rule, medicine is *practiced*. That term is not arbitrary. Medicine is a constantly changing art as we learn more and more about genetics, electronic aids (like CAT scans and MRIs) and daily laboratory advances. There are many dog maladies, like canine hip dysplasia, which are not universally treated in the same manner. Some veterinarians opt for surgery more often than others do.

SELECTING A QUALIFIED VET

Your selection of a veterinarian should be based not only upon personality and ability with large dogs but also upon his convenience to your home. You want a vet who is close because you might have emergencies or need to make multiple visits for treatments. You want a vet who has services that you might require such as tattooing and grooming facilities, as well as sophisticated pet supplies and a good reputation for ability and responsiveness. There is nothing more frustrating than having to wait a day or more to get a response from your veterinarian.

All veterinarians are licensed and their diplomas and/or certificates should be displayed in their waiting rooms. There are,

Before you buy a dog, meet and interview the vets in your area. Take everything into consideration; discuss background, specialties, fees, emergency policies, etc.

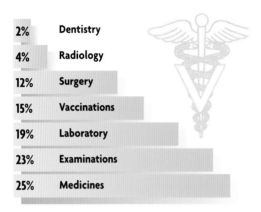

2%	Dentistry
4%	Radiology
12%	Surgery
15%	Vaccinations
19%	Laboratory
23%	Examinations
25%	Medicines

A typical vet's income, categorized according to services performed. This survey dealt with small-animal (pets) practices.

however, many veterinary specialties that usually require further studies and internships. There are specialists in heart problems (veterinary cardiologists), skin problems (veterinary dermatologists), teeth and gum problems (veterinary dentists), eye problems (veterinary ophthalmologists), x-rays (veterinary radiologists) and vets who have specialties in bones, muscles or certain organs. Most veterinarians do routine surgery such as neutering, stitching up wounds and docking tails for those breeds in which such is required for show purposes. When the problem affecting your dog is serious, it is not unusual or impudent to get another medical opinion. You might also want to compare costs among several veterinarians. Sophisticated health care and veterinary services can be very costly. Important decisions are often based upon financial considerations.

PREVENTATIVE MEDICINE

It is much easier, less costly and more effective to practice preventative medicine than to fight bouts of illness and disease. Properly bred puppies come from parents that were selected based upon their genetic-disease profiles. Their dam should have been vaccinated, free of all internal and external parasites, and properly nourished. For these reasons, a visit to the veterinarian who cared for the dam is recommended. The dam can pass on disease resistance to her puppies, which can last for eight to ten weeks. She can also pass on parasites and many infections. That's why you should learn as much about the dam as possible.

WEANING TO FIVE MONTHS OLD

Puppies should be weaned by the time they are about two months old. A puppy that remains for at least eight weeks with his dam

NEUTERING/SPAYING

Male dogs are castrated. The operation removes both testicles and requires that the dog be anesthetized. Recovery takes about one week. Females are spayed; in this operation, the uterus (womb) and both of the ovaries are removed. This is major surgery, also carried out under general anesthesia, and it usually takes a bitch two weeks to recover.

First Aid at a Glance

Burns
Place the affected area under cool water; use ice if only a small area is burnt.

Bee stings/Insect bites
Apply ice to relieve swelling; antihistamine dosed properly.

Animal bites
Clean any bleeding area; apply pressure until bleeding subsides; go to the vet.

Spider bites
Use cold compress and a pressurized pack to inhibit venom's spreading.

Antifreeze poisoning
Induce vomiting with hydrogen peroxide. Seek *immediate* veterinary help!

Fish hooks
Removal best handled by vet; hook must be cut in order to remove.

Snake bites
Pack ice around bite; contact vet quickly; identify snake for proper antivenin.

Car accident
Move dog from roadway with blanket; seek veterinary aid.

Shock
Calm the dog; keep him warm; seek immediate veterinary help.

Nosebleed
Apply cold compress to the nose; apply pressure to any visible abrasion.

Bleeding
Apply pressure above the area; treat wound by applying a cotton pack.

Heat stroke
Submerge dog in cold bath; cool down with fresh air and water; go to the vet.

Frostbite/Hypothermia
Warm the dog with a warm bath, electric blankets or hot water bottles.

Abrasions
Clean the wound and wash out thoroughly with fresh water; apply antiseptic.

 Remember: an injured dog may attempt to bite a helping hand from fear and confusion. Always muzzle the dog before trying to offer assistance.

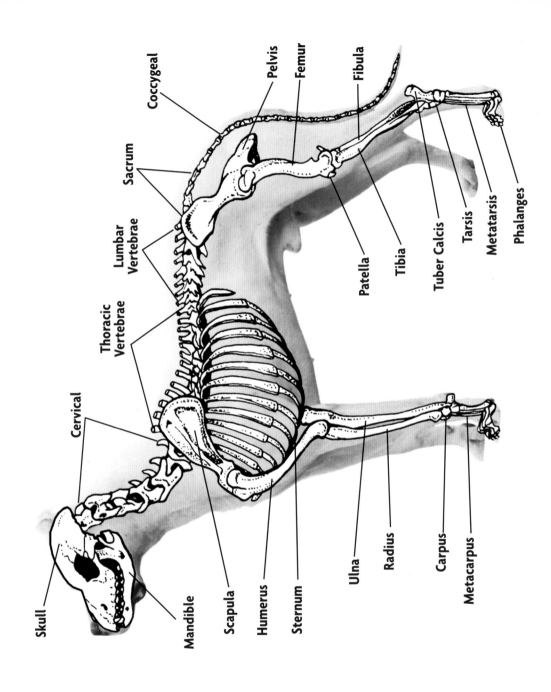

Skeletal Structure of the Dogo Argentino

and littermates usually adapts better to other dogs and people later in his life.

In every case, you should have your newly acquired puppy examined by a veterinarian immediately. Vaccination programs usually begin when the puppy is very young.

The puppy will have his teeth examined and have his skeletal conformation and general health checked prior to certification by the veterinarian. Many puppies have problems with their kneecaps, cataracts and other eye problems, heart murmurs and undescended testicles. They may also have personality problems and your vet might have training in temperament evaluation.

VACCINATION SCHEDULING

Most vaccinations are given by injection and should only be done by a veterinarian. Both he and you should keep a record of the date of the injection, the identification of the vaccine and the amount given. Some vets give a first vaccination at eight weeks, but most dog breeders prefer the course not to commence until about ten weeks because of negating any antibodies passed on by the dam. The vaccination scheduling is usually based on a 15-day cycle. You must take your vet's advice as to when to vaccinate as this may differ according to the vaccine used. Most vaccinations immu-

BE CAREFUL WHERE YOU WALK YOUR DOG

Dogs who have been exposed to lawns sprayed with herbicides have double and triple the rate of malignant lymphoma. Suburban dogs are especially at risk, as they are exposed to manicured lawns and gardens. Dogs perspire and absorb through their footpads. Be careful where your dog walks and always avoid any area that appears yellowed from chemical overspray. These chemicals are not good for you, either!

nize your puppy against viruses.

The usual vaccines contain immunizing doses of several different viruses such as distemper, parvovirus, parainfluenza and hepatitis. There are other vaccines available when the puppy is at risk. You should rely upon professional advice. This is especially true for the booster-shot program. Most vaccination programs require a booster when the puppy is a year old and once a year thereafter. In some cases, circumstances may require more or less frequent immunizations. Canine cough, more formally known as tracheobronchitis, is treated with a vaccine that is sprayed into the dog's nostrils. Canine cough is usually included in routine vaccination, but this is often not so effective as for other major diseases.

HEALTH AND VACCINATION SCHEDULE

AGE IN WEEKS:	6TH	8TH	10TH	12TH	14TH	16TH	20-24TH	52ND
Worm Control	✔	✔	✔	✔	✔	✔	✔	
Neutering							✔	
Heartworm		✔		✔		✔	✔	
Parvovirus	✔		✔		✔		✔	✔
Distemper		✔		✔		✔		✔
Hepatitis		✔		✔		✔		✔
Leptospirosis								✔
Parainfluenza	✔		✔		✔			✔
Dental Examination		✔					✔	✔
Complete Physical		✔					✔	✔
Coronavirus				✔			✔	✔
Canine Cough	✔							
Hip Dysplasia								✔
Rabies							✔	

Vaccinations are not instantly effective. It takes about two weeks for the dog's immune system to develop antibodies. Most vaccinations require annual booster shots. Your vet should guide you in this regard.

FIVE MONTHS TO ONE YEAR OF AGE
By the time your puppy is five months old, he should have completed his vaccination program. During his physical examination he should be evaluated for the common hip dysplasia and other diseases of the joints. There are tests to assist in the prediction of these problems. Other tests can be run to assess the effectiveness of the vaccination program.

Unless you intend to breed or show your dog, neutering the puppy at six months of age is recommended. Discuss this with your veterinarian; most professionals advise neutering the puppy. Neutering has proven to be extremely beneficial to both male and female dogs. Besides eliminating the possibility of pregnancy, it inhibits (but does not prevent) breast cancer in bitches and prostate cancer in male dogs.

Your veterinarian should provide your puppy with a thorough dental evaluation at six months of age, ascertaining whether all of the permanent teeth have erupted properly. A home dental-care regimen should be initiated at six months, including brushing weekly and providing good dental devices (such as nylon bones). Regular dental-care promotes healthy teeth, fresh breath and a longer life.

OVER ONE YEAR OF AGE

Once a year, your grown dog should visit the vet for an examination and vaccination boosters. Some vets recommend blood tests, thyroid level check and dental evaluation to accompany these annual visits. A thorough clinical evaluation by the vet can provide critical background information for your dog. Blood tests are often performed at one year of age, and dental examinations around the third or fourth birthday. In the long run, quality preventative care for your pet can save money, teeth and lives.

SKIN PROBLEMS IN DOGO ARGENTINOS

Veterinarians are consulted by dog owners for skin problems more than any other group of diseases or maladies. Dogs' skin is almost

DISEASE REFERENCE CHART

	What is it?	What causes it?	Symptoms
Leptospirosis	Severe disease that affects the internal organs; can be spread to people.	A bacterium, which is often carried by rodents, that enters through mucous membranes and spreads quickly throughout the body.	Range from fever, vomiting and loss of appetite in less severe cases to shock, irreversible kidney damage and possibly death in most severe cases.
Rabies	Potentially deadly virus that infects warm-blooded mammals.	Bite from a carrier of the virus, mainly wild animals.	1st stage: dog exhibits change in behavior, fear. 2nd stage: dog's behavior becomes more aggressive. 3rd stage: loss of coordination, trouble with bodily functions.
Parvovirus	Highly contagious virus, potentially deadly.	Ingestion of the virus, which is usually spread through the feces of infected dogs.	Most common: severe diarrhea. Also vomiting, fatigue, lack of appetite.
Canine cough	Contagious respiratory infection.	Combination of types of bacteria and virus. Most common: *Bordetella bronchiseptica* bacteria and parainfluenza virus.	Chronic cough.
Distemper	Disease primarily affecting respiratory and nervous system.	Virus that is related to the human measles virus.	Mild symptoms such as fever, lack of appetite and mucus secretion progress to evidence of brain damage, "hard pad."
Hepatitis	Virus primarily affecting the liver.	Canine adenovirus type I (CAV-1). Enters system when dog breathes in particles.	Lesser symptoms include listlessness, diarrhea, vomiting. More severe symptoms include "blue-eye" (clumps of virus in eye).
Coronavirus	Virus resulting in digestive problems.	Virus is spread through infected dog's feces.	Stomach upset evidenced by lack of appetite, vomiting, diarrhea.

DENTAL HEALTH

A dental examination is in order when the dog is between six months and one year of age so that any permanent teeth that have erupted incorrectly can be corrected. It is important to begin a brushing routine, preferably using a two-sided brushing technique, whereby both sides of the tooth are brushed at the same time. Durable nylon and safe edible chews should be a part of your puppy's arsenal for good health, good teeth and pleasant breath. The vast majority of dogs three to four years old and older has diseases of the gums from lack of dental attention. Using the various types of dental chews can be very effective in controlling dental plaque.

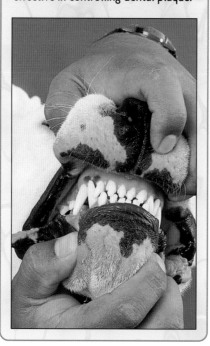

as sensitive as human skin and both suffer from almost the same ailments, though the occurrence of acne in dogs is rare! For this reason, veterinary dermatology has developed into a specialty practiced by many veterinarians.

Since many skin problems have visual symptoms that are almost identical, it requires the skill of an experienced veterinary dermatologist to identify and cure many of the more severe skin disorders. Pet shops sell many treatments for skin problems but most of the treatments are directed at symptoms and not the underlying problem(s). If your dog is suffering from a skin disorder, you should seek professional assistance as quickly as possible. As with all diseases, the earlier a problem is identified and treated, the more successful is the cure.

HEREDITARY SKIN DISORDERS

Veterinary dermatologists are currently researching a number of skin disorders that are believed to have hereditary bases. These inherited diseases are transmitted by both parents, who appear (phenotypically) normal but have a recessive gene for the disease, meaning that they carry, but are not affected by, the disease. These diseases pose serious problems to breeders because in some instances there is no method of identifying carriers. Often the secondary diseases associated with these skin conditions are even more debilitating than the skin disorder, including cancers and respiratory problems.

Among the known hereditary skin disorders, for which the mode of inheritance is known, are acrodermatitis, cutaneous asthenia (Ehlers-Danlos syndrome), sabaceous adenitis, cyclic hematopoiesis, dermatomyositis, IgA deficiency, color dilution alopecia and nodular dermatofibrosis. Some of these disorders are limited to one or two breeds and others affect a large number of breeds. All inherited diseases must be diagnosed and treated by a veterinary specialist.

PARASITE BITES

Many of us are allergic to mosquito bites. The bites itch, erupt and may even become infected. Dogs have the same reaction to fleas, ticks and/or mites. When you feel the prick of the mosquito as it bites you, you have a chance to kill it with your hand. Unfortunately, when your dog is bitten by a flea, tick or mite, he can only scratch it away or bite it. By the time the dog has been bitten, the parasite has done some of its damage. It may also have laid eggs to cause further problems in the near future. The itching from parasite bites is probably due to the saliva injected into the site when the parasite sucks the dog's blood.

AUTO-IMMUNE SKIN CONDITIONS

Auto-immune skin conditions are commonly referred to as being allergic to yourself, while allergies are usually inflammatory reactions to an outside stimulus. Auto-immune diseases cause serious damage to the tissues that are involved.

The best known auto-immune disease is lupus, which affects people as well as dogs. The symptoms are variable and may affect the kidneys, bones, blood chemistry and skin. It can be fatal to both dogs and humans, though it is not thought to be transmissible. It is usually successfully treated with cortisone, prednisone or similar corticosteroid, but extensive use of these drugs can have harmful side effects.

AIRBORNE ALLERGIES

Just as humans have hay fever, rose fever and other fevers from which they suffer during the pollinating season, many dogs suffer from the same allergies.

MORE THAN VACCINES

Vaccinations help prevent your new puppy from contracting diseases, but they do not cure them. Proper nutrition as well as parasite control keep your dog healthy and less susceptible to many dangerous diseases. Remember that your dog depends on you to ensure his well-being.

12 WAYS TO PREVENT BLOAT

Gastric torsion or bloat is a preventable killer of dogs. We know that bloat affects more large dogs and deep-chested dogs than any other dogs. Bloat can be defined as the rapid accumulation of air in the stomach, causing it to twist or flip over, thereby blocking the entrance and exit. A dog suffering from bloat experiences acute pain and is unable to release the gas. Here are some excellent recommendations to prevent this life-threatening condition.

- Do not provide water at mealtimes, especially for dogs that commonly drink large amounts of water.
- Keep your dog at his proper weight. Avoid overfeeding.
- Limit exercise at least one hour before and two hours after mealtime.
- Avoid stressful or vigorous exercise altogether.
- Provide antacids for any dog with audible stomach motions (borborygmus) or flatulence.
- Feed two or three smaller meals instead of one large meal per day.
- Serve your dog's food and water on a bowl stand so that he does not have to crane his neck to eat.
- Never allow the dog to gulp water.
- Be certain that mealtime is a non-stressful time. Feed the dog alone where he is not competing with a canine or feline housemate for his bowl. Feeding the dog in his crate is an excellent solution.
- For the big gulper, place large toys in the dog's bowl so that he cannot gulp his portions.
- Discuss bloat prevention and preventative surgical methods with your veterinarian.
- If changing your dog's diet, do so gradually.
- Recognize the symptoms of bloat, as time is of the essence. Symptoms include pacing, whining, wretching (with no result), groaning, obvious discomfort.

When the pollen count is high, your dog might suffer but don't expect him to sneeze and have a runny nose like a human would. Dogs react to pollen allergies the same way they react to fleas—they scratch and bite themselves. Dogo Argentinos are very susceptible to airborne pollen allergies.

Dogs, like humans, can be tested for allergens. Discuss the testing with your veterinary dermatologist.

FOOD ALLERGIES

Dogs may be allergic to many foods that are best-sellers and highly recommended by breeders and veterinarians. Changing the brand of food that you buy may not eliminate the problem if the element to which the dog is allergic is contained in the new brand.

Recognizing a food allergy is difficult. Humans vomit or have rashes when they eat a food to which they are allergic. Dogs neither vomit nor (usually) develop a rash. They react in the same manner as they do to an airborne or flea allergy: they itch, scratch and bite, thus making the diagnosis extremely difficult. While pollen allergies and parasite bites are usually seasonal, food allergies are year-round problems.

Food Intolerance

Food intolerance is the inability of the dog to completely digest certain foods. For example, puppies that may have done very well on their mother's milk may not do well on cow's milk. The result of this food intolerance may be loose bowels, passing gas and stomach pains. These are the only obvious symptoms of food intolerance and that makes diagnosis very difficult.

Treating Food Problems

It is possible to handle food allergies and food intolerance yourself. Put your dog on a diet that he has never had. Obviously if he has never eaten this new food he can't have been allergic or intolerant of it. Start with a single ingredient that is not in the dog's diet at the present time. Ingredients like chopped beef or chicken are common in dog's diets, so try something more exotic like rabbit, pheasant or some other source of protein. Keep the dog on this diet (with no additives) for a month. If the symptoms of food allergy or intolerance disappear, chances are your dog has a food allergy.

Don't think that the single ingredient cured the problem. You still must find a suitable diet and ascertain which ingredient in the old diet was objectionable. This is most easily done by adding ingredients to the new diet one at a time. Let the dog stay on the modified diet for a month before you add another ingredient. Eventually, you will determine the ingredient that caused the adverse reaction.

An alternative method is to study the ingredients in the diet to which your dog is allergic or intolerant. Identify the main ingredient in this diet and eliminate it by buying a different food that does not have that ingredient. Keep experimenting until the symptoms disappear after one month.

This picturesque landscape could be a nightmare for your Dogo. Some Dogos are allergic to flower pollen. They usually react by scratching, not sneezing.

A male dog flea, *Ctenocephalides canis.*

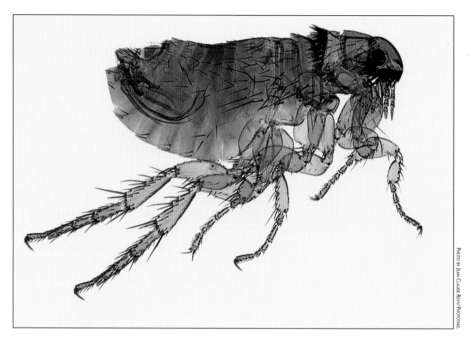

PHOTO BY JEAN CLAUDE REVY/PHOTOTAKE

EXTERNAL PARASITES

FLEAS

Of all the problems to which dogs are prone, none is more well known and frustrating than fleas. Flea infestation is relatively simple to cure but difficult to prevent. Parasites that are harbored inside the body are a bit more difficult to eradicate but they are easier to control.

To control flea infestation, you have to understand the flea's life cycle. Fleas are often thought of as a summertime problem, but centrally heated homes have changed the patterns and fleas can be found at any time of the year. The most effective method of flea control is a two-stage approach: one stage to kill the adult fleas, and the other to control the development of pre-adult fleas. Unfortunately, no single active ingredient is effective against all stages of the life cycle.

FLEA KILLER CAUTION— "POISON"

Flea-killers are poisonous. You should not spray these toxic chemicals on areas of a dog's body that he licks, including his genitals and his face. Flea killers taken internally are a better answer, but check with your vet in case internal therapy is not advised for your dog.

LIFE CYCLE STAGES

During its life, a flea will pass through four life stages: egg, larva, pupa or nymph and adult. The adult stage is the most visible and irritating stage of the flea life cycle, and this is why the majority of flea-control products concentrate on this stage. The fact is that adult fleas account for only 1% of the total flea population, and the other 99% exist in pre-adult stages, i.e., eggs, larvae and nymphs. The pre-adult stages are barely visible to the naked eye.

THE LIFE CYCLE OF THE FLEA

Eggs are laid on the dog, usually in quantities of about 20 or 30, several times a day. The adult female flea must have a blood meal before each egg-laying session. When first laid, the eggs will cling to the dog's hair, as the eggs are still moist. However, they will quickly dry out and fall from the dog, especially if the dog moves around or scratches. Many eggs will fall off in the dog's favorite area or an area in which he spends a lot of time, such as his bed.

Once the eggs fall from the dog onto the carpet or furniture, they will hatch into larvae. This takes from one to ten days. Larvae are not particularly mobile and will usually travel only a few inches from where they hatch. However, they do have a tendency to move away from bright light and heavy

---

EN GARDE: CATCHING FLEAS OFF GUARD!

Consider the following ways to arm yourself against fleas:

- Add a small amount of pennyroyal or eucalyptus oil to your dog's bath. These natural remedies repel fleas.
- Supplement your dog's food with fresh garlic (minced or grated) and a hearty amount of brewer's yeast, both of which ward off fleas.
- Use a flea comb on your dog daily. Submerge fleas in a cup of bleach to kill them quickly.
- Confine the dog to only a few rooms to limit the spread of fleas in the home.
- Vacuum daily...and get all of the crevices! Dispose of the bag every few days until the problem is under control.
- Wash your dog's bedding daily. Cover cushions where your dog sleeps with towels, and wash the towels often.

---

traffic—under furniture and behind doors are common places to find high quantities of flea larvae.

The flea larvae feed on dead organic matter, including adult flea feces, until they are ready to change into adult fleas. Fleas will usually remain as larvae for around seven days. After this period, the larvae will pupate into protective pupae. While inside the pupae, the larvae will undergo metamorphosis and change into

PHOTO BY DWIGHT R. KUHN

Fleas have been measured as being able to jump 300,000 times and can jump over 150 times their length in any direction, including straight up.

adult fleas. This can take as little time as a few days, but the adult fleas can remain inside the pupae waiting to hatch for up to two years. The pupae are signaled to hatch by certain stimuli, such as physical pressure—the pupae's being stepped on, heat from an animal's lying on the pupae or increased carbon-dioxide levels and vibrations—indicating that a suitable host is available.

Once hatched, the adult flea must feed within a few days. Once the adult flea finds a host, it will not leave voluntarily. It only becomes dislodged by grooming or the host animal's scratching. The adult flea will remain on the

host for the duration of its life unless forcibly removed.

TREATING THE ENVIRONMENT AND THE DOG

Treating fleas should be a two-pronged attack. First, the environment needs to be treated; this includes carpets and furniture, especially the dog's bedding and areas underneath furniture. The environment should be treated with a household spray containing an Insect Growth Regulator (IGR) and an insecticide to kill the adult fleas. Most IGRs are effective against eggs and larvae; they actually mimic the fleas' own hormones and stop the eggs and larvae from developing into adult fleas. There are currently no treatments available to attack the pupa stage of the life cycle, so the adult insecticide is used to kill the newly hatched adult fleas before they find a host. Most IGRs are active for many months, while adult insecticides are only active

A scanning electron micrograph of a dog or cat flea, *Ctenocephalides*, magnified more than 100x. This image has been colorized for effect.

S. E. M. BY DR DENNIS KUNKEL, UNIVERSITY OF HAWAII.

THE LIFE CYCLE OF THE FLEA

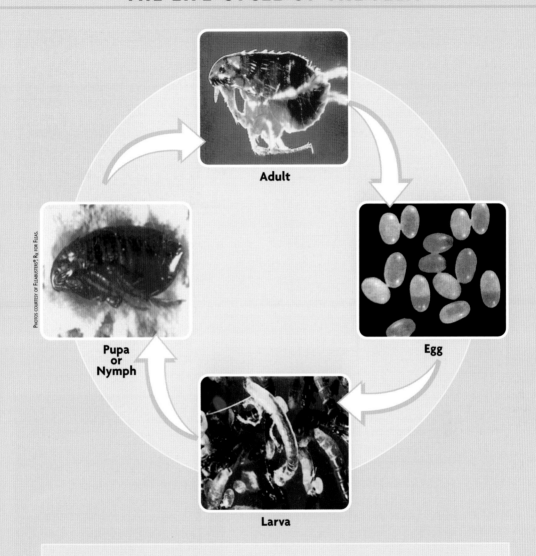

Adult

Egg

Larva

Pupa
or
Nymph

PHOTOS COURTESY OF FLEABUSTERS® Rx FOR FLEAS.

Fleas have been around for millions of years and have adapted to
changing host animals. They are able to go through a complete life cycle
in less than one month or they can extend their lives to almost two years
by remaining as pupae or cocoons. They do not need blood or any other
food for up to 20 months.

INSECT GROWTH REGULATOR (IGR)

Two types of products should be used when treating fleas—a product to treat the pet and a product to treat the home. Adult fleas represent less than 1% of the flea population. The pre-adult fleas (eggs, larvae and pupae) represent more than 99% of the flea population and are found in the environment; it is in the case of pre-adult fleas that products containing an Insect Growth Regulator (IGR) should be used in the home.

IGRs are a new class of compounds used to prevent the development of insects. They do not kill the insect outright, but instead use the insect's biology against it to stop it from completing its growth. Products that contain methoprene are the world's first and leading IGRs. Used to control fleas and other insects, this type of IGR will stop flea larvae from developing and protect the house for up to seven months.

The American dog tick, *Dermacentor variabilis*, is probably the most common tick found on dogs. Look at the strength in its eight legs! No wonder it's hard to detach them.

is to apply an adult insecticide to the dog. Traditionally, this would be in the form of a collar or a spray, but more recent innovations include digestible insecticides that poison the fleas when they ingest the dog's blood. Alternatively, there are drops that, when placed on the back of the dog's neck, spread throughout the hair and skin to kill adult fleas.

TICKS

Though not as common as fleas, ticks are found all over the tropical and temperate world. They don't bite, like fleas; they harpoon. They dig their sharp proboscis (nose) into the dog's skin and drink the blood. Their only food and drink is dog's for a few days.

When treating with a household spray, it is a good idea to vacuum before applying the product. This stimulates as many pupae as possible to hatch into adult fleas. The vacuum cleaner should also be treated with an insecticide to prevent the eggs and larvae that have been collected in the vacuum bag from hatching.

The second stage of treatment

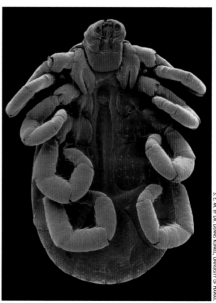

S. E. M. BY DR. DENNIS KUNKEL, UNIVERSITY OF HAWAII

blood. Dogs can get Lyme disease, Rocky Mountain spotted fever, tick bite paralysis and many other diseases from ticks. They may live where fleas are found and they like to hide in cracks or seams in walls. They are controlled the same way fleas are controlled.

The American dog tick, *Dermacentor variabilis*, may well be the most common dog tick in many geographical areas, especially those areas where the climate is hot and humid. Most dog ticks have life expectancies of a week to six months, depending upon climatic conditions. They can neither jump nor fly, but they can crawl slowly and can range up to 16 feet to reach a sleeping or unsuspecting dog.

MITES

Just as fleas and ticks can be problematic for your dog, mites can also lead to an itchy nuisance. Microscopic in size, mites are related to ticks and generally take up permanent residence on their host animal—in this case, your dog! The term *mange* refers to any infestation caused by one of the mighty mites, of which there are six varieties that concern dog owners.

Demodex mites cause a condition known as demodicosis (sometimes called red mange or

DEER-TICK CROSSING
The great outdoors may be fun for your dog, but it also is a home to dangerous ticks. Deer ticks carry a bacterium known as *Borrelia burgdorferi* and are most active in the autumn and spring. When infections are caught early, penicillin and tetracycline are effective antibiotics, but, if left untreated, the bacteria may cause neurological, kidney and cardiac problems as well as long-term trouble with walking and painful joints.

S. E. M. BY DR. ANDREW SPIELMAN/PHOTOTAKE.

PHOTO BY DR. DENNIS KUNKEL, UNIVERSITY OF HAWAII.

The head of an American dog tick, *Dermacentor variabilis*, enlarged and colorized for effect.

The mange mite, *Psoroptes bovis*, can infest cattle and other domestic animals.

PHOTO BY JAMES HAYDEN/YOAV/PHOTOTAKE.

follicular mange), in which the mites live in the dog's hair follicles and sebaceous glands in larger-than-normal numbers. This type of mange is commonly passed from the dam to her puppies and usually shows up on the puppies' muzzles, though demodicosis is not transferable from one normal dog to another. Most dogs recover from this type of mange without any treatment, though topical therapies are commonly prescribed by the vet.

The *Cheyletiellosis* mite is the hook-mouthed culprit associated

Human lice look like dog lice; the two are closely related.

PHOTO BY DWIGHT R. KUHN.

with "walking dandruff," a condition that affects dogs as well as cats and rabbits. This mite lives on the surface of the animal's skin and is readily transferable through direct or indirect contact with an affected animal. The dandruff is present in the form of scaly skin, which may or may not be itchy. If not treated, this mange can affect a whole kennel of dogs and can be spread to humans as well.

The *Sarcoptes* mite causes intense itching on the dog in the form of a condition known as scabies or sarcoptic mange. The cycle of the *Sarcoptes* mite lasts about three weeks, and the mites live in the top layer of the dog's skin (epidermis), preferably in areas with little hair. Scabies is highly contagious and can be passed to humans. Sometimes an allergic reaction to the mite worsens the severe itching associated with sarcoptic mange.

Ear mites, *Otodectes cynotis,* lead to otodectic mange, which most commonly affects the outer ear canal of the dog, though other areas can be affected as well. Dogs with ear-mite infestation commonly scratch at their ears, causing further irritation, and shake their heads. Dark brown droppings in the outer ear confirm the diagnosis. Your vet can prescribe a treatment to flush out the ears and kill any eggs in the ears. A complete month of treatment is necessary to cure the mange.

Two other mites, less common in dogs, include *Dermanyssus gallinae* (the poultry or red mite) and *Eutrombicula alfreddugesi* (the North American mite associated with trombiculidiasis or chigger infestation). The poultry mite frequently lives on chickens, but can transfer to dogs who spend time near farm animals. Chigger infestation affects dogs in the

DO NOT MIX
Never mix parasite-control products without first consulting your vet. Some products can become toxic when combined with others and can cause fatal consequences.

NOT A DROP TO DRINK
Never allow your dog to swim in polluted water or public areas where water quality can be suspect. Even perfectly clear water can harbor parasites, many of which can cause serious to fatal illnesses in canines. Areas inhabited by waterfowl and other wildlife are especially dangerous.

Central US who have exposure to woodlands. The types of mange caused by both of these mites are treatable by vets.

INTERNAL PARASITES
Most animals—fishes, birds and mammals, including dogs and humans—have worms and other parasites that live inside their bodies. According to Dr. Herbert R. Axelrod, the fish pathologist, there are two kinds of parasites: dumb and smart. The smart parasites live in peaceful cooperation with their hosts (symbiosis), while the dumb parasites kill their hosts. Most worm infections are relatively easy to control. If they are not controlled, they weaken the host dog to the point that other medical problems occur, but they do not kill the host as dumb parasites would.

A brown dog tick, *Rhipicephalus sanguineus*, is an uncommon but annoying tick found on dogs.

Photo by Carolina Biological Supply/Phototake.

The roundworm *Rhabditis* can infect both dogs and humans.

ROUNDWORMS

Average-size dogs can pass 1,360,000 roundworm eggs every day. For example, if there were only 1 million dogs in the world, the world would be saturated with thousands of tons of dog feces. These feces would contain around 15,000,000,000 roundworm eggs.

Up to 31% of home yards and children's sand boxes in the US contain roundworm eggs.

Flushing dog's feces down the toilet is not a safe practice because the usual sewage treatments do not destroy roundworm eggs.

Infected puppies start shedding roundworm eggs at three weeks of age. They can be infected by their mother's milk.

The roundworm, *Ascaris lumbricoides.*

ROUNDWORMS

The roundworms that infect dogs are known scientifically as *Toxocara canis.* They live in the dog's intestines and shed eggs continually. It has been estimated that a dog produces about 6 or more ounces of feces every day. Each ounce of feces averages hundreds of thousands of roundworm eggs. There are no known areas in which dogs roam that do not contain roundworm eggs. The greatest danger of roundworms is that they infect people, too! It is wise to have your dog tested regularly for roundworms.

In young puppies, roundworms cause bloated bellies, diarrhea, coughing and vomiting, and are transmitted from the dam (through blood or milk). Affected puppies will not appear as animated as normal puppies. The worms appear spaghetti-like, measuring as long as 6 inches. Adult dogs can acquire roundworms through coprophagia (eating contaminated feces) or by killing rodents that carry roundworms.

Roundworm infection can kill puppies and cause severe problems in adults, as the hatched larvae travel to the lungs and trachea through the bloodstream. Cleanliness is the best preventative for roundworms. Always pick up after your dog and dispose of feces in appropriate receptacles.

Photo by Dwight R. Kuhn.

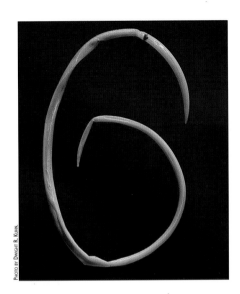

PHOTO BY DWIGHT R. KUHN.

HOOKWORMS

In the United States, dog owners have to be concerned about four different species of hookworm, the most common and most serious of which is *Ancylostoma caninum,* which prefers warm climates. The others are *Ancylostoma braziliense, Ancylostoma tubaeforme* and *Uncinaria stenocephala,* the latter of which is a concern to dogs living in the Northern US and Canada, as this species prefers cold climates. Hookworms are dangerous to humans as well as to dogs and cats, and can be the cause of severe anemia due to iron deficiency. The worm uses its teeth to attach itself to the dog's intestines and changes the site of its attachment about six times per day. Each time the worm repositions itself, the dog loses blood and can become anemic. *Ancylostoma caninum* is the most likely of the four species to cause anemia in the dog.

Symptoms of hookworm infection include dark stools, weight loss, general weakness, pale coloration and anemia, as well as possible skin problems. Fortunately, hookworms are easily purged from the affected dog with a number of medications that have proven effective. Discuss these with your vet. Most heartworm preventatives include a hookworm insecticide as well.

Owners also must be aware that hookworms can infect humans, who can acquire the larvae through exposure to contaminated feces. Since the worms cannot complete their life cycle on a human, the worms simply infest the skin and cause irritation. This condition is known as cutaneous larva migrans syndrome. As a preventative, use disposable gloves or a "poop-scoop" to pick up your dog's droppings and prevent your dog (or neighborhood cats) from defecating in children's play areas.

The hookworm, *Ancylostoma caninum.*

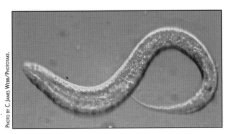

PHOTO BY C. JAMES WEBB/PHOTOTAKE.

The infective stage of the hookworm larva.

TAPEWORMS

Humans, rats, squirrels, foxes, coyotes, wolves and domestic dogs are all susceptible to tapeworm infection. Except in humans, tapeworms are usually not a fatal infection. Infected individuals can harbor 1000 parasitic worms.

Tapeworms, like some other types of worm, are hermaphroditic, meaning male and female in the same worm.

If dogs eat infected rats or mice, or anything else infected with tapeworm, they get the tapeworm disease. One month after attaching to a dog's intestine, the worm starts shedding eggs. These eggs are infective immediately. Infective eggs can live for a few months without a host animal.

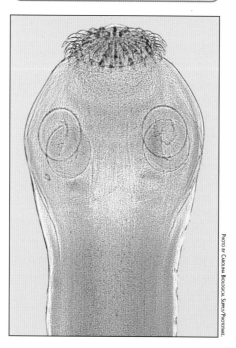

The head and rostellum (the round prominence on the scolex) of a tapeworm, which infects dogs and humans.

PHOTO BY CAROLINA BIOLOGICAL SUPPLY/PHOTOTAKE.

TAPEWORMS

There are many species of tapeworm, all of which are carried by fleas! The most common tapeworm affecting dogs is known as *Dipylidium caninum*. The dog eats the flea and starts the tapeworm cycle. Humans can also be infected with tapeworms—so don't eat fleas! Fleas are so small that your dog could pass them onto your hands, your plate or your food and thus make it possible for you to ingest a flea that is carrying tapeworm eggs.

While tapeworm infection is not life-threatening in dogs (smart parasite!), it can be the cause of a very serious liver disease for humans. About 50% of the humans infected with *Echinococcus multilocularis*, a type of tapeworm that causes alveolar hydatid, perish.

WHIPWORMS

In North America, whipworms are counted among the most common parasitic worms in dogs. The whipworm's scientific name is *Trichuris vulpis*. These worms attach themselves in the lower parts of the intestine, where they feed. Affected dogs may only experience upset tummies, colic and diarrhea. These worms, however, can live for months or years in the dog, beginning their larval stage in the small intestine, spending their adult stage in the large intestine and finally passing infective eggs through the dog's feces. The only way to detect whipworms is through a fecal examination, though this is not always foolproof. Treatment for whipworms is tricky, due to the worms' unusual life-cycle pattern, and very often dogs are reinfected due to exposure to infective eggs on the ground. The whipworm eggs can survive in the environment for as long as five years; thus, cleaning up droppings in your own backyard as well as in public places is essential for sanitation purposes and the health of your dog and others.

THREADWORMS
Though less common than round-worms, hookworms and those previously mentioned, thread-

worms concern dog owners in the Southwestern US and Gulf Coast area where the climate is hot and humid. Living in the small intes-tine of the dog, this worm measures a mere 2 millimeters and is round in shape. Like that of the whipworm, the threadworm's life cycle is very complex and the eggs and larvae are passed through the feces. A deadly disease in humans, *Strongyloides* readily infects people, and the handling of feces is the most common means of trans-mission. Threadworms are most often seen in young puppies; bloody diarrhea and pneumonia are symptoms. Sick puppies must be isolated and treated immedi-ately; vets recommend a follow-up treatment one month later.

HEARTWORM PREVENTATIVES

There are many heartworm preventatives on the market, many of which are sold at your veterinarian's office. These products can be given daily or monthly, depending on the manufacturer's instructions. All of these preventatives contain chemical insecticides directed at killing heartworms, which leads to some controversy among dog owners. In effect, heartworm preventatives are neces-sary evils, though you should determine how necessary based on your pet's lifestyle. There is no doubt that heartworm is a dreadful disease that threatens the lives of dogs. However, the likelihood of your dog's being bitten by an infected mosquito is slim in most places, and a mosquito-repellent (or an herbal remedy such as Wormwood or

Black Walnut) is much safer for your dog and will not compromise his immune system (the way heartworm preventatives will). Should you decide to use the tradi-tional preventative "medications," you can consider giving the pill every other or third month. Since the toxins in the pill will kill the heartworms at all stages of develop-ment, the pill would be effective in killing larvae, nymphs or adults, and it takes four months for the larvae to reach the adult stage. Thus, there is no rationale to poison-ing the dog's system on a monthly basis. Lastly, do not give the pill during the winter months, since there are no mosquitoes around to pass on their infection, unless you live in a tropical environment.

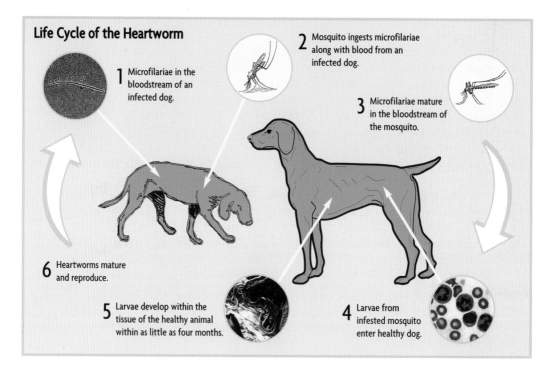

Life Cycle of the Heartworm

1 Microfilariae in the bloodstream of an infected dog.

2 Mosquito ingests microfilariae along with blood from an infected dog.

3 Microfilariae mature in the bloodstream of the mosquito.

6 Heartworms mature and reproduce.

5 Larvae develop within the tissue of the healthy animal within as little as four months.

4 Larvae from infested mosquito enter healthy dog.

HEARTWORMS

Heartworms are thin, extended worms up to 12 inches long, which live in a dog's heart and the major blood vessels surrounding it. Dogs may have up to 200 worms. Symptoms may be loss of energy, loss of appetite, coughing, the development of a pot belly and anemia.

Heartworms are transmitted by mosquitoes. The mosquito drinks the blood of an infected dog and takes in larvae with the blood. The larvae, called microfilariae, develop within the body of the mosquito and are passed on to the next dog bitten after the larvae mature. It takes two to three weeks for the larvae to develop to the infective stage within the body of the mosquito. Dogs are usually treated at about six weeks of age and maintained on a prophylactic dose given monthly.

Blood testing for heartworms is not necessarily indicative of how seriously your dog is infected. Although this is a dangerous disease, it is not easy for a dog to be infected. Discuss the various preventatives with your vet, as there are many different types now available. Together you can decide on a safe course of prevention for your dog.

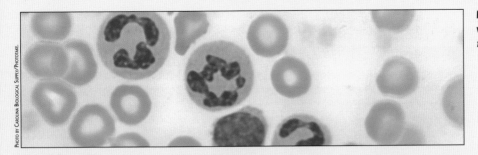

Magnified heartworm larvae, *Dirofilaria immitis.*

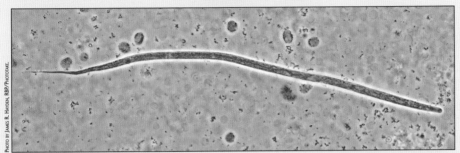

Heartworm, *Dirofilaria immitis.*

The heart of a dog infected with canine heartworm, *Dirofilaria immitis.*

HOMEOPATHY:
an alternative
to conventional
medicine

"Less is Most"

Using this principle, the strength of a homeopathic remedy is measured by the number of serial dilutions that were undertaken to create it. The greater the number of serial dilutions, the greater the strength of the homeopathic remedy. The potency of a remedy that has been made by making a dilution of 1 part in 100 parts (or 1/100) is 1c or 1cH. If this remedy is subjected to a series of further dilutions, each one being 1/100, a more dilute and stronger remedy is produced. If the remedy is diluted in this way six times, it is called 6c or 6cH. A dilution of 6c is 1 part in 1,000,000,000,000. In general, higher potencies in more frequent doses are better for acute symptoms and lower potencies in more infrequent doses are more useful for chronic, long-standing problems.

CURING OUR DOGS NATURALLY

Holistic medicine means treating the whole animal as a unique, perfect, living being. Generally, holistic treatments do not suppress the symptoms that the body naturally produces, as do most medications prescribed by conventional doctors and vets. Holistic methods seek to cure disease by regaining balance and harmony in the patient's environment. Some of these methods include use of nutritional therapy, herbs, flower essences, aromatherapy, acupuncture, massage, chiropractic and, of course, the most popular holistic approach, homeopathy.

Homeopathy is a theory or system of treating illness with small doses of substances which, if administered in larger quantities, would produce the symptoms that the patient already has. This approach is often described as "like cures like." Although modern veterinary medicine is geared toward the "quick fix," homeopathy relies on the belief that, given the time, the body is able to heal itself and return to its natural, healthy state.

Choosing a remedy to cure a problem in our dogs is the difficult part of homeopathy. Consult with your vet for a professional diagnosis of your dog's symptoms. Often

these symptoms require immediate conventional care. If your vet is willing and knowledgeable, you may attempt a homeopathic remedy. Be aware that cortisone prevents homeopathic remedies from working. There are hundreds of possibilities and combinations to cure many problems in dogs, from basic physical problems such as excessive shedding, fleas or other parasites, unattractive doggy odor, bad breath, upset tummy, obesity, dry, oily or dull coat, diarrhea, ear problems or eye discharge (including tears and dry or mucousy matter), to behavioral abnormalities such as fear of loud noises, habitual licking, poor appetite, excessive barking and various phobias. From alumina to zincum metallicum, the remedies span the planet and the imagination...from flowers and weeds to chemicals, insect droppings, diesel smoke and volcanic ash.

Using "Like to Treat Like"

Unlike conventional medicines that suppress symptoms, homeopathic remedies treat illnesses with small doses of substances that, if administered in larger quantities, would produce the symptoms that the patient already has. While the same homeopathic remedy can be used to treat different symptoms in different dogs, here are some interesting remedies and their uses.

Apis Mellifica
(made from honey bee venom) can be used for allergies or to reduce swelling that occurs in acutely infected kidneys.

Diesel Smoke
can be used to help control travel sickness.

Calcarea Fluorica
(made from calcium fluoride, which helps harden bone structure) can be useful in treating hard lumps in tissues.

Natrum Muriaticum
(made from common salt, sodium chloride) is useful in treating thin, thirsty dogs.

Nitricum Acidum
(made from nitric acid) is used for symptoms you would expect to see from contact with acids, such as lesions, especially where the skin joins the linings of body orifices or openings such as the lips and nostrils.

Symphytum
(made from the herb Knitbone, *Symphytum officianale*) is used to encourage bones to heal.

Urtica Urens
(made from the common stinging nettle) is used in treating painful, irritating rashes.

DOGO ARGENTINO

The term *old* is a qualitative term. For dogs, as well as their masters, old is relative. Certainly we can all distinguish between a puppy Dogo Argentino and an adult Dogo Argentino—there are the obvious physical traits, such as size, appearance and facial expressions, and personality traits. Puppies and young dogs like to play with children. Children's natural exuberance is a good match for the seemingly endless energy of young dogs. They like to run, jump, chase and retrieve. When dogs grow and cease their interaction with children, they are often thought of as being too old to play with them.

On the other hand, if a Dogo Argentino is only exposed to people with quieter lifestyles, his life will normally be less active and he will not seem to be getting old as his activity level slows down.

If people live to be 100 years old, dogs live to be 20 years old. While this is a good rule of thumb, it is very inaccurate. When trying to compare dog years to human years, you cannot make a generalization about all dogs. You can make the generalization that 12 years is a good lifespan for a Dogo Argentino, which is quite good compared to many other large pure-bred dogs that may only live to 8 or 9 years of age. Some Dogo Argentinos have been known to live to longer. Dogs are generally considered mature within three years, but they can reproduce even earlier. So the first three years of a dog's life are like seven times that of comparable humans. That means a 3-year-old dog is like a 21-year-old human. As the curve of comparison shows, there is no hard and fast rule for comparing dog and human ages. The comparison is made even more difficult, for not all humans age at the same rate...and human females live longer than human males.

WHAT TO LOOK FOR IN SENIORS

Most vets and behaviorists use the seven-year mark as the time to consider a dog a senior. The term *senior* does not imply that the dog is geriatric and has begun to fail in mind and body. Aging is essentially a slowing process. Humans readily admit that they feel a difference in their activity level from age 20 to 30, and then from 30 to 40, etc. By treating the seven-year-old dog as a senior, owners are able to implement certain therapeutic and preventative medical strategies with the help of their vets. A senior-care program should include at least two veterinary visits per year, screening sessions to determine the dog's health status, as well as nutritional counseling. Vets determine the senior dog's health status through a blood smear for a complete blood count, serum chemistry profile with electrolytes, urinalysis, blood pressure check, electrocardiogram, ocular tonometry (pressure on the eyeball) and dental prophylaxis.

Such an extensive program for

GETTING OLD

The bottom line is simply that your dog is getting old when you think he is getting old because he slows down in his level of general activity, including walking, running, eating, jumping and retrieving. On the other hand, the frequency of certain activities increases, such as more sleeping, more barking and more repetition of habits like going to the door without being called when you put your coat on to leave the house.

senior dogs is well advised before owners start to see the obvious physical signs of aging, such as slower and inhibited movement, graying, increased sleep/nap

Senior Dogos will be less active and playful than their younger counterparts. Two Dogos growing old together can make the golden years more pleasant.

period, and disinterest in play and other activity. This preventative program promises a longer, healthier life for the aging dog. Among the physical problems common in aging dogs are the loss of hearing and vision, arthritis, kidney and liver failure, diabetes mellitus, heart disease and Cushing's disease (a hormonal disease).

In addition to the physical manifestations discussed, there are some behavioral changes and problems related to aging dogs. Dogs suffering from hearing or vision loss, dental discomfort or arthritis can become aggressive. Likewise the near-deaf and/or blind dog may be startled more easily and react in an unexpect-

edly aggressive manner. Seniors suffering from senility can become more impatient and irritable. Housesoiling accidents are associated with loss of mobility, kidney problems, loss of sphincter control as well as plaque accumulation, physiological brain changes and reactions to medications. Older dogs, just like young puppies, suffer from separation anxiety, which can lead to excessive barking, whining, housesoiling and destructive behavior. Seniors may become fearful of everyday sounds, such as vacuum cleaners, heaters, thunder and passing traffic. Some dogs have difficulty sleeping, due to discomfort, the need for frequent potty

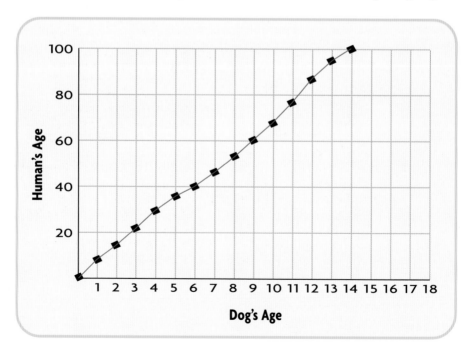

CDS: COGNITIVE DYSFUNCTION SYNDROME
"Old-Dog Syndrome"

There are many ways for you to evaluate old-dog syndrome. Veterinarians have defined CDS (cognitive dysfunction syndrome) as the gradual deterioration of cognitive abilities. These are indicated by changes in the dog's behavior. When a dog changes his routine response, and maladies have been eliminated as the cause of these behavioral changes, then CDS is the usual diagnosis.

More than half the dogs over eight years old suffer from some form of CDS. The older the dog, the more chance he has of suffering from CDS. In humans, doctors often dismiss the CDS behavioral changes as part of "winding down."

There are four major signs of CDS: frequent potty accidents inside the home, sleeping much more or much less than normal, acting confused and failing to respond to social stimuli.

SYMPTOMS OF CDS

FREQUENT POTTY ACCIDENTS
- *Urinates in the house.*
- *Defecates in the house.*
- *Doesn't signal that he wants to go out.*

SLEEP PATTERNS
- *Moves much more slowly.*
- *Sleeps more than normal during the day.*
- *Sleeps less during the night.*

CONFUSION
- *Goes outside and just stands there.*
- *Appears confused with a faraway look in his eyes.*
- *Hides more often.*
- *Doesn't recognize friends.*
- *Doesn't come when called.*
- *Walks around listlessly and without a destination.*

FAILURE TO RESPOND TO SOCIAL STIMULI
- *Comes to people less frequently, whether called or not.*
- *Doesn't tolerate petting for more than a short time.*
- *Doesn't come to the door when you return home.*

visits and the like. Owners should avoid spoiling the older dog with too many fatty treats. Obesity is a common problem in older dogs and subtracts years from their lives. Keep the senior dog as trim as possible since excessive weight puts additional stress on the body's vital organs. Some breeders recommend supplementing the diet with foods high in fiber and lower in calories. Adding fresh vegetables and marrow broth to the senior's diet makes a tasty, low-calorie, low-fat supplement. Vets also offer specialty diets for senior dogs that are worth exploring.

Your dog, as he nears his twilight years, needs his owner's patience and good care more than ever. Never punish an older dog for an accident or abnormal

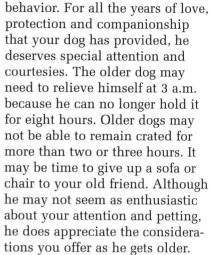

behavior. For all the years of love, protection and companionship that your dog has provided, he deserves special attention and courtesies. The older dog may need to relieve himself at 3 a.m. because he can no longer hold it for eight hours. Older dogs may not be able to remain crated for more than two or three hours. It may be time to give up a sofa or chair to your old friend. Although he may not seem as enthusiastic about your attention and petting, he does appreciate the considerations you offer as he gets older.

Your Dogo Argentino does not understand why his world is slowing down. Owners must make the transition into the golden years as pleasant and rewarding as possible.

WHAT TO DO WHEN THE TIME COMES

You are never fully prepared to make a rational decision about putting your dog to sleep. It is very obvious that you love your Dogo Argentino or you would not be reading this book. Putting a loved dog to sleep is extremely difficult. It is a decision that must be made with your veterinarian. You are usually forced to make the decision when one of the life-threatening symptoms listed above becomes serious enough for you to seek veterinary help.

If the prognosis of the malady indicates the end is near and your

SENIOR SIGNS

An old dog starts to show one or more of the following symptoms:

- The hair on the face and paws starts to turn gray.
- Sleep patterns are deeper and longer, and the old dog is harder to awaken.
- Food intake diminishes.
- Responses to calls, whistles and other signals are ignored more and more.
- Eye contact does not evoke tail wagging (assuming it once did).

beloved pet will only suffer more and experience no enjoyment for the balance of his life, then euthanasia is the right choice.

WHAT IS EUTHANASIA?

Euthanasia derives from the Greek, meaning *good death*. In other words, it means the planned, painless killing of a dog suffering from a painful, incurable condition, or who is so aged that he cannot walk, see, eat or control his excretory functions.

Euthanasia is usually accomplished by injection with an overdose of an anesthesia or barbiturate. Aside from the prick of the needle, the experience is usually painless.

MAKING THE DECISION

The decision to euthanize your dog is never easy. The days during which the dog becomes ill and the end occurs can be unusually stressful for you. If this is your first experience with the death of a loved one, you may need the comfort dictated by your religious beliefs. If you are the head of the family and have children, you should have involved them in the decision of putting your Dogo Argentino to sleep. Usually your dog can be maintained on drugs for a few days in order to give you ample time to make a decision. During this time, talking with members of the family or religious representatives, or even people

who have lived through this same experience, can ease the burden of your inevitable decision. In any case, euthanasia is painful and stressful for the family of the dog. Unfortunately, it does not end there.

THE FINAL RESTING PLACE

Dogs can have some of the same privileges as humans. They can occasionally be buried in their entirety in a pet cemetery which is generally expensive, or they can be buried on your property in

NOTICING THE SYMPTOMS

The symptoms listed below are symptoms that gradually appear and become more noticeable. They are not life-threatening; however, the symptoms below are to be taken very seriously and warrant a discussion with your veterinarian:

- Your dog cries and whimpers when he moves, and he stops running completely.
- Convulsions start or become more serious and frequent. The usual convulsion (spasm) is when the dog stiffens and starts to tremble, being unable or unwilling to move. The seizure usually lasts for 5 to 30 minutes.
- Your dog drinks more water and urinates more frequently. Wetting and bowel accidents take place indoors without warning.
- Vomiting becomes more and more frequent.

When you are ready, you may choose to share your life with a new bundle of Argentine love—a new Dogo puppy!

a place suitably marked with some stone or newly planted tree or bush. Alternatively, they can be cremated and the ashes returned to you, or some people prefer to leave their dogs at the vet's office for the vet to dispose of.

EUTHANASIA
Euthanasia must be performed by a licensed veterinarian. There also may be societies for the prevention of cruelty to animals in your area. They often offer this service upon a vet's recommendation.

All of these options should be discussed frankly and openly with your veterinarian. Do not be afraid to ask financial questions. Cremations can be individual, but a less expensive option is mass cremation, although of course the ashes can not then be returned. Vets can usually arrange cremation services on your behalf.

GETTING ANOTHER DOG?
The grief of losing your beloved dog will be as lasting as the grief of losing a human friend or relative. In most cases, if your dog died of old age (if there is such a

thing), he had slowed down considerably. Do you want a new Dogo Argentino puppy to replace it? Or are you willing to rescue a more mature Dogo Argentino, say two to three years of age, which will usually be house-trained and will have an already developed personality? This avenue is equally challenging to raising a new Dogo pup, but perhaps even more rewarding.

The decision is, of course, your own. Do you want another Dogo Argentino or perhaps a different breed so as to avoid comparison with your beloved friend? Most people usually buy the same breed because they know and love the characteristics of that breed. Then, too, they often know people who have the same breed and perhaps they are lucky enough that a breeder they know and respect expects a litter soon. What could be better?

Many pet cemeteries have facilities for storing a dog's ashes.

Consult your veterinarian to help you locate a pet cemetery in your area.

No matter how similar this line-up of Dogos appears, every Dogo is different. While some generalizations can be substantiated, behaviorists treat each dog as an individual.

DOGO ARGENTINO

As a Dogo Argentino owner, you have selected your dog so that you and your loved ones can have a companion, a protector, a friend and a four-legged family member. You invest time, money and effort to care for and train the family's new charge. Of course, this chosen canine behaves perfectly! Well, perfectly like a dog. When discussing the Dogo Argentino, owners have much to consider.

THINK LIKE A DOG

Dogs do not think like humans, nor do humans think like dogs, though we try. Unfortunately, a dog is incapable of figuring out how humans think, so the responsibility falls on the owner to adopt a proper canine mindset. Dogs cannot rationalize, and dogs exist in the present moment. Many dog owners make the mistake in training of thinking that they can reprimand their dog for something he did a while ago. Basically, you cannot even reprimand a dog for something he did 20 seconds ago! Either catch him in the act or forget it! It is a waste of your and your dog's time—in his mind, you are reprimanding

him for whatever he is doing at that moment.

The following behavioral problems represent some which owners most commonly encounter. Every dog is unique and every situation is unique. No author could purport for you to solve your Dogo Argentino's problem simply by reading a chapter

NO KISSES

We all love our dogs and our dogs love us. They show their love and affection by licking us. This is not a very sanitary practice, as dogs lick and sniff in some unsavory places. Kissing your dog on the mouth is strictly forbidden, as parasites can be transmitted in this manner.

in a breed book. Here we outline some basic "dogspeak" so that owners' chances of solving behavioral problems are increased. Discuss bad habits with your veterinarian and he can recommend a behavioral specialist to consult in appropriate cases. Since behavioral abnormalities are the leading reason owners abandon their pets, we hope that you will make a valiant effort to solve your Dogo Argentino's problem. Patience and understanding are virtues that must dwell in every pet-loving household.

AGGRESSION

This is the most obvious problem that concerns owners of Dogo

Dogos can be trained as attack dogs, but this sort of training is not advised because the Dogo is a naturally protective animal. Sharpening these skills is highly discouraged.

Argentinos. Aggression can be a very big problem in dogs, but more so in a dog with a fighting background. Aggression, when not controlled, always becomes dangerous. An aggressive dog, no matter the size, may lunge at, bite or even attack a person or another dog. Aggressive behavior is not to be tolerated. It is more than just inappropriate behavior; it is not safe, especially with a tenacious, powerful breed such as the Dogo Argentino. It is painful for a family to watch their dog become unpredictable in his behavior to the point where they are afraid of him. While not all aggressive behavior is dangerous, growling, baring teeth and the like can be frightening. It is important to ascertain why the dog is acting in this manner. Aggression is a display of dominance, and the dog should not have the dominant role in his pack, which is, in this case, your family.

It is important not to challenge an aggressive dog as this could provoke an attack. Observe your Dogo Argentino's body language. Does he make direct eye contact and stare? Does he try to make himself as large as possible: ears pricked, chest out, tail erect? Height and size signify authority in a dog pack—being taller or "above" another dog literally means that he is "above" in the social status. These body signals tell you that your Dogo

Argentino thinks he is in charge, a problem that needs to be addressed. An aggressive dog is unpredictable: you never know when he is going to strike and what he is going to do. You cannot understand why a dog that is playful and loving one minute is growling and snapping the next.

The best solution is to consult a behavioral specialist, one who has experience with the Dogo Argentino if possible. Together, perhaps you can pinpoint the cause of your dog's aggression and do something about it. An aggressive dog cannot be trusted, and a dog that cannot be trusted is not safe to have as a family pet. If, very unusually, you find that your pet has become untrustworthy and you feel it necessary to seek a new home with a more suitable family and environment, explain fully to the new owners all your reasons for rehoming the dog to be fair to all concerned. In the very worst case, you will have to consider euthanasia.

I'M HOME!
Dogs left alone for varying lengths of time may often react wildly when their owners return. Sometimes they run, jump, bite, chew, tear things apart, wet themselves, gobble their food or behave in very undisciplined ways. If your dog behaves in this manner upon your return home, allow him to calm down before greeting him or he will consider your attention as a reward for his antics.

AGGRESSION TOWARD OTHER DOGS
A dog's aggressive behavior toward another dog sometimes stems from insufficient exposure to other dogs at an early age. If other dogs make your Dogo Argentino nervous and agitated, he may lash out as a defensive mechanism. A dog who has not received sufficient exposure to other canines tends to believe that he is the only dog on the planet. The animal becomes so dominant that he does not even show signs that he is fearful or threatened. Without growling or any other physical signal as a warning, he will lunge at and bite the other dog. A way to correct

Only experienced handlers should attempt sleeve training with a Dogo.

dog wants to dominate those under him and please those above him. Dogs know that there must be a leader. If you are not the obvious choice for emperor, the dog will assume the throne! These conflicting innate desires are what a dog owner is up against when he sets about training a dog. In training a dog to obey commands, the owner is reinforcing that he is the top dog in the "pack" and that the dog should, and should want to, serve his superior. Thus, the owner is suppressing the dog's urge to dominate by modifying his behavior and making him obedient.

An important part of training is taking every opportunity to reinforce that you are the leader. The simple action of making your Dogo Argentino sit to wait for his food says that you control when he eats and that he is dependent on you for food. Although it may be difficult, do not give in to your dog's wishes every time he whines at you or looks at you with his pleading eyes. It is a constant effort to show the dog that his place in the pack is at the bottom. This is not meant to sound cruel or inhumane. You love your Dogo Argentino and you should treat him with care and affection. You most likely did not get a dog just so you could boss around another creature. Dog training is not about being cruel

this is to let your Dogo Argentino approach another dog when walking on lead. Watch very closely and at the very first sign of aggression, correct your Dogo Argentino and pull him away. Scold him for any sign of discomfort, and then praise him when he ignores or tolerates the other dog. Keep this up until he stops the aggressive behavior, learns to ignore the other dog or accepts other dogs. Praise him lavishly for his correct behavior.

DOMINANT AGGRESSION
A social hierarchy is firmly established in a wild dog pack. The

or feeling important, it is about molding the dog's behavior into what is acceptable and teaching him to live by your rules. In theory, it is quite simple: catch him in appropriate behavior and reward him for it. Add a dog into the equation and it becomes a bit more trying, but as a rule of thumb, positive reinforcement is what works best.

With a dominant dog, punishment and negative reinforcement can have the opposite effect of what you are after. It can make a dog fearful and/or act out aggressively if he feels he is being challenged. Remember, a dominant dog perceives himself at the top of the social heap and will fight to defend his perceived status. The best way to prevent that is never to give him reason to think that he is in control in the first place. If you are having trouble training your Dogo Argentino and it seems as if he is constantly challenging your authority, seek the help of an obedience trainer or behavioral specialist. A professional will work with both you and your dog to teach you effective techniques to use at home. Beware of trainers who rely on excessively harsh methods; scolding is necessary now and then, but the focus in your training should always be on positive reinforcement.

If you can isolate what brings out the fear reaction, you can help the dog get over it. Supervise your Dogo Argentino's interactions with people and other dogs, and praise the dog when it goes well. If he starts to act aggressively in a situation, correct him and remove him from the situation. Do not let people approach the dog and start petting him without your express permission. That way, you can have the dog sit to accept petting, and praise him when he behaves properly. You are focusing on praise and on modifying his behavior by rewarding him when he acts appropriately. By being gentle and by supervising his interactions, you are showing him that there is no need to be afraid or defensive.

SEXUAL BEHAVIOR
Dogs exhibit certain sexual behaviors that may have influenced your choice of male or female when you first purchased your Dogo. To a certain extent, spaying/neutering will eliminate these behaviors, but if you are purchasing a dog that you wish to breed, you should be aware of what you will have to deal with throughout the dog's life.

Female dogs usually have two estruses per year with each season lasting about three weeks. These are the only times in which a female dog will mate, and she usually will not allow this until the second week of the cycle, but this does vary from bitch to bitch.

If not bred during the heat cycle, a bitch may experience a false pregnancy, in which her mammary glands swell and she exhibits maternal tendencies toward toys or other objects.

Owners must further recognize that mounting is not merely a sexual expression but also one of dominance. Be consistent and persistent and you will find that you can "move mounters."

CHEWING

Dogs need to chew, to massage their gums, to make their new teeth feel better and to exercise their jaws. This is a natural behavior deeply imbedded in all things canine. Your role as owner is not to stop the dog's chewing, but to redirect it to positive, chew-worthy objects. Be an informed owner and purchase proper chew toys like strong nylon bones that will not splinter. Be sure that the devices are safe and durable, since your dog's safety is at risk. Again, the owner is responsible for ensuring a dog-proof environment. The best answer is prevention: that is, put your shoes, handbags and other tasty objects in their proper places (out of the reach of the growing canine mouth). Direct puppies to their toys whenever you see them tasting the furniture legs or the leg of your pants. Make a loud noise to attract the pup's attention and immediately

DOGGIE DEMOCRACY

Your dog inherited the pack-leader mentality. He only knows about pecking order. He instinctively wants to be top dog, but you have to convince him that you are boss. There is no such thing as living in a democracy with your dog. You are the one who makes the rules.

NO JUMPING

Stop a dog from jumping up before he jumps. If he is getting ready to jump onto you, simply walk away. If he jumps up on you before you can turn away, lift your knee so that it bumps him in the chest. Do not be forceful. Your dog soon will realize that jumping up is not a productive way of getting attention.

Pick a command such as "Off" (avoid using "Down" since you will use that for the dog to lie down) and tell him "Off" when he jumps up. Place him on the ground on all fours and have him sit, praising him the whole time. Always lavish him with praise and petting when he is in the sit position.

escort him to his chew toy and engage him with the toy for at least four minutes, praising and encouraging him all the while.

Some trainers recommend deterrents, such as hot pepper or another bitter spice or a product designed for this purpose, to discourage the dog from chewing unwanted objects. Test these products on your Dogo before investing in a large quantity.

DIGGING

Digging, which is seen as a destructive behavior to humans, is actually quite a natural behavior in dogs. Although your Dogo is not one of the "earth dogs" (also known as terriers), his desire to dig can be irrepressible and most frustrating to his owners. Dogos enjoy digging more than some terriers do, and are very good at it! When digging occurs in your yard, it is actually a normal behavior redirected into something the dog can do in his everyday life. In the wild, a dog would be actively seeking food, making his own shelter, etc. He would be using his paws in a purposeful manner for his survival. Since you provide him with food and shelter, he has no need to use his paws for these purposes, and so the energy that he would be using may manifest itself in the form of little holes all over your yard and flower beds.

Basically, the answer is to provide the dog with adequate play and exercise so that his mind and paws are occupied, and so that he feels as if he is doing something useful. Digging is easiest to control if it is stopped as soon as possible, but it is often hard to catch a dog in the act. If your dog is a compulsive digger and is not easily distracted by other activities, you can designate an area on your property where it is okay for him to dig. If you catch him digging in an off-limits area of the yard, immediately bring him to the approved area and praise him for digging there. Keep a close eye on him so that you can catch him in the act—

that is the only way to make him understand what is permitted and what is not.

BARKING

Dogos are not barkers—it is not their nature as hunters to use their voices very often. Sometimes a Dogo will bark to warn his owner about something he feels is worth announcing, but this never becomes a problem. It is only when the barking becomes excessive, and when the excessive barking becomes a bad habit, that the behavior needs to be modified. Fortunately, Dogo Argentinos use their barks more purposefully than most other dogs; most dogs are not as discriminate as the Dogo Argentino.

If an intruder came into your home in the middle of the night and your Dogo Argentino barked a warning, wouldn't you be pleased? You would probably deem your dog a hero, a wonderful guardian and protector of the home. However, if a friend drops by unexpectedly and rings the doorbell and is greeted with a sudden sharp bark, you would probably be annoyed at the dog. But in reality, isn't this just the same behavior? The dog does not know any better. Unless he sees who is at the door and it is someone he knows, he will bark as a means of vocalizing that his (and your) territory is being threatened. While your friend is not posing a threat, it is all the same to the dog. Barking is his means of letting you know that there is an intrusion, whether friend or foe, on your property. This type of barking is instinctive and should not be discouraged.

Excessive habitual barking, however, is a problem that should be corrected early on. As your Dogo Argentino grows up, you will be able to tell when his barking is purposeful and when it is for no reason. You will become able to distinguish your dog's different barks and their meanings. For example, the bark when someone comes to the door will be different than the bark when he is excited to see you. It is similar to a person's tone of voice, except that the dog has to rely totally on tone of voice because he does not have the

DOG TALK

Deciphering your dog's barks is very similar to understanding a baby's cries: there is a different cry for eating, sleeping, potty needs, etc. Your dog talks to you not only through howls and groans but also through his body language. Baring teeth, staring and inflating the chest are all threatening gestures. If a dog greets you by licking his nose, turning his head or yawning, these are friendly, peacemaking gestures.

HE'S PROTECTING YOU

Barking is your dog's way of protecting you. If he barks at a stranger walking past your house, a moving car or a fleeing cat, he is merely exercising his responsibility to protect his pack (YOU) and territory from a perceived intruder. Since the "intruder" usually keeps going, the dog thinks his barking chased it away and he feels fulfilled. This behavior leads your overly vocal friend to believe that he is the "dog in charge."

benefit of using words. An incessant barker will be evident at an early age.

There are some things that encourage a dog to bark. For example, if your dog barks non-stop for a few minutes and you give him a treat to quiet him, he believes that you are rewarding him for barking. He will associate barking with getting a treat, and will keep doing it until he is rewarded.

FOOD STEALING

Is your dog devising ways of stealing food from your coffee table? If so, you must answer the following questions: Is your Dogo Argentino hungry, or is he "constantly famished" like many dogs seem to be? Face it, some dogs are more food-motivated than others. Some dogs are totally obsessed by the smell of food and can only think of their next meal. Food stealing is terrific fun and always yields a great reward—*food*, glorious food.

The owner's goal, therefore, is to be sensible about where food is placed in the home, and to reprimand your dog whenever caught in the act of stealing. But remember, only reprimand the dog if you actually see him stealing, not later when the crime is discovered for that will be of no use at all and will only serve to confuse.

BEGGING

Just like food stealing, begging is a favorite pastime of hungry puppies! It yields that same tasty reward—*food!* Dogs quickly learn that their owners keep the "good food" for ourselves, and that we humans do not dine on dry food alone. Begging is a conditioned response related to a specific stimulus, time and place. The sounds of the kitchen, cans and bottles opening, crinkling bags, the smell of food in preparation, etc., will excite the dog and soon the paws are in the air!

Here is the solution to stopping this behavior: Never give in to a beggar! You are rewarding the dog for sitting pretty, jumping up, whining and rubbing his nose into you by giving him that glorious reward—food. By ignoring the dog, you will (eventually) force the behavior into extinction. Note that the behavior likely gets worse before it disappears, so be sure there are not any "softies" in the family who will give in to little "Olivero" every time he whimpers, *"Más, por favor."*

SEPARATION ANXIETY

Your Dogo Argentino may howl, whine or otherwise vocalize his displeasure at your leaving the house and his being left alone. This is a normal reaction, no different than the child who cries as his mother leaves him on the first day at school. In fact, constant attention can lead to separation anxiety in the first place. If you are endlessly fussing over your dog, he will come to expect this from you all of the time and it will be more traumatic for him when you are not there. Obviously, you enjoy spending time with your dog, and he thrives on your love and attention. However, it should not become a dependent relationship in which he is heartbroken without you.

One thing you can do to minimize separation anxiety is to make your entrances and exits as low-key as possible. Do not give your dog a long drawn-out goodbye, and do not lavish him with hugs and kisses when you return. This is giving in to the attention that he craves, and it will only make him miss it more when you

are away. Another thing you can try is to give your dog a treat when you leave; this will not only keep him occupied and keep his mind off the fact that you have just left, but it will also help him associate your leaving with a pleasant experience.

You may have to accustom your dog to being left alone in intervals. Of course, when your dog starts whimpering as you approach the door, your first instinct will be to run to him and comfort him, but do not do it! Really—eventually he will adjust and be just fine if you take it in small steps. His anxiety stems from being placed in an unfamiliar situation; by familiarizing him with being alone he will learn that he is okay. That is not to say you should purposely leave your dog home alone, but the dog needs to know that while he can depend on you for his care, you do not have to be by his side 24 hours a day.

When the dog is alone in the house, he should be confined to his designated dog-proof area of the house. This should be the area in which he sleeps and already feels comfortable so he will feel more at ease when he is alone.

COPROPHAGIA

Feces eating is, to most humans, one of the most disgusting behaviors that a dog could engage in, yet to the dog it is perfectly normal. It is hard for us to understand why a dog would want to eat his own feces. He could be seeking certain nutrients that are missing from his diet; he could be just plain hungry; or he could be attracted by the pleasing (to a dog) scent. While coprophagia most often refers to the dog eating his own feces, a dog may just as likely eat that of another animal if he comes across it. Dogs often find the stool of cats and horses more palatable than that of other dogs.

Vets have found that diets with a low digestibility, containing relatively low levels of fiber and high levels of starch, increase coprophagia. Therefore, high-fiber diets may decrease the likelihood of dogs eating feces. Both the consistency of the stool (how firm it feels in the dog's mouth) and the presence of undigested nutrients increase the likelihood. Once the dog develops diarrhea from feces eating, he will likely quit this distasteful habit.

To discourage this behavior, first make sure that the food you are feeding your dog is nutritionally complete and that he is getting enough food. If changes in his diet do not seem to work, and no medical cause can be found, you will have to modify the behavior before it becomes a habit through environmental control. The best way to prevent

your dog from eating his stool is to make it unavailable—clean up after he eliminates and remove any stool from the yard. If it is not there, he cannot eat it.

Reprimanding for stool eating rarely impresses the dog. Veterinarians recommend distracting the dog while he is in the act of stool eating. Coprophagia is seen most frequently in pups 6 to 12 months of age, and usually disappears around the dog's first birthday.

NO BUTTS ABOUT IT!

Dogs get to know each other by sniffing each other's backsides. It seems that each dog has a telltale odor, probably created by the anal glands. It also distinguishes sex and signals when a female will be receptive to a male's attention. Some dogs snap at another dog's intrusion of their private parts.

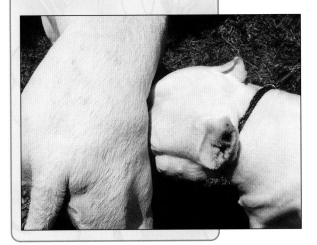

INDEX

*Page numbers in **boldface** indicate illustrations.*

My Dogo Argentino

PUT YOUR PUPPY'S FIRST PICTURE HERE

Dog's Name _____

Date _____ Photographer _____